T0067783

SOCIAL MEDIA MUSINGS

Book 3

GEORGE WAAS

authorHOUSE®

AuthorHouse™
1663 Liberty Drive
Bloomington, IN 47403
www.authorhouse.com
Phone: 833-262-8899

Published by AuthorHouse 09/14/2022

ISBN: 978-1-6655-7089-3 (sc)
ISBN: 978-1-6655-7088-6 (e)

Print information available on the last page.

This book is printed on acid-free paper.

CONTENTS

INTRODUCTION

In 2022, I wrote a book titled "Social Media Musings." In the introduction, I said I am the product of two professions driven by inquiry and skepticism, journalism, and law.

I noted that both professions are founded upon logic, rational thinking, critical analysis, and sound judgment. So, when I see something that doesn't make sense, defies logic, is irrational, or otherwise off-the-wall, I ask questions and search for answers.

I also confessed that I am a Facebook junkie, although not necessarily enamored with social media. There is certainly far too much misinformation, flat-out wrong information, etc., being spread on social media. And we know that "a lie travels around the globe while the truth is putting on its shoes."

In that book, I said that, for the most part, I kept my opinions to myself, or shared them with family and friends, until the January 6, 2021, attack on our nation's capital. Since then, taking to heart the note on the Facebook page that says, "What's on your mind," I've posted my thoughts and opinions about various situations on a variety of subjects. Many of my posts are quite lengthy, solely because of the importance I place on fact, analysis, reason, logic, critical thinking, and sound judgment.

I then included in my book, in chronological order from January 6, 2021, to February 2022, my posts on a variety of subjects, mostly—but certainly not all— on politics. Since that book was published in March 2022, I continued to post of Facebook, hoping to continue a national dialog on issues of great public importance, which resulted in Book 2, which was also published in 2022. But I didn't stop there.

Here is Book 3 of my social media musings on Facebook.

A SIMPLE SOLUTION TO THE ABORTION DEBATE

Now that abortion is no longer a constitutional right, here is a simple solution that serves the interests of both the pro-choice and pro-life supporters.

Adoption.

The Supreme Court's decision doesn't require the birth mother to actually care for the baby after birth. She can simply give it up for adoption. All she has to do is make it clear as early as possible that she doesn't want to keep the baby. When she arrives at the hospital, or even if she delivers elsewhere, her declaration will be clear. And there are enough providers out there that will honor her declaration.

Reproductive rights groups can easily make available to the community the names, addresses and phone numbers of all Evangelical churches in the area. They can even go online and find the names, home addresses and phone numbers of the church leaders. These folks are so pro-life and so rigidly Republican, they obviously believe in individual responsibility and accountability. They will surely step up and welcome these babies into their homes and churches. After all, since they burdened women who now can't abort their fetuses, these churchgoers will step up to the plate and resolve the crisis they created through their rigid demands of their equally rigid politicians and justices. They created the problem; they're on the hook for a solution. That's the Republican mantra, right?

Of course, we know these Bible thumpers are against any legislation that might provide a lifeline of assistance after birth, like childcare, tax credits, food programs, aid to new mothers, etc. Can't have government intruding into our private lives, or have others pay for these women who happened to become pregnant with an unwanted child. Of course, government can intrude into the lives of women who want an abortion, but that really doesn't count to these self-professed moralists on the extreme right.

But it's a new day now, thanks to the 27% rock-ribbed conservatives who oppose abortion at all costs. These folks are caring, loving, nurturing people who really can't wait to take in these babies, and gleefully raise them to be future Evangelicals.

And we know that, even if they are not of a mind to adopt, they will use their vast network of foster homes to provide loving care and nurturing until a permanent home is found.

We can even extend this opportunity to the governors and legislators of the several states who've either outlawed abortion or are about to. Get those names, addresses and phone numbers and circulate them throughout these several states. Think of all those who will stand up, do the right thing and adopt these precious, wanted babies!

And if you believe this, there is some great oceanfront property in Nebraska that's your for a steal.

PRAYER ON THE 50-YARD LINE—SUPREME COURT DECISION

If this coach prayed in his office, or in some private place, I would have no problem with that. But he chose to pray on the 50-yard line after a football game, with who knows how many in the stands. His students felt obligated to join him. In fact, this wasn't an isolated situation. This coach routinely did this over an eight-year period, with students regularly joining him. There is at least a latent form of coach-student influence at play here. Further, school officials told him he couldn't do this. The 50-yard line is not a proper place for personal, private prayer.

Next time you're in FSU's Campbell Stadium, do you think you'll see a Catholic, Muslim, etc., praying on the logo? Maybe the next time someone in the Donald Tucker Civic Center becomes so overwhelmed with the result of the game, he'll go to mid-court and offer up a prayer of thanks for victory. Or maybe after the next baseball game on TV, the winning manager will go to the mound or home plate and offer up his thanks. The point here is that once religion gets its foot in the door, the rest of the body will follow. I fully understand that there are two sides involved here. Some see this as benign; I don't. Others see it as the further blurring of the line between church and state; I do.

Once they overlap, or they are absorbed into each other, when church and state become one, well, just look at Saudi Arabia, Afghanistan, Pakistan, etc.

TRUMP AIDE'S TESTIMONY DAMNING

I remember Alexander Butterfield's shocking testimony almost 50 years ago that President Nixon, under investigation for Watergate, taped his conversations. I thought that was the single most revelatory testimony about a crooked president in our nation's history. Until June 28, 2022. Trump's Chief of Staff Mark Meadows' top aide, Cassidy Hutchinson, who testified before the House select committee investigating the January 6 attack on the capital, offered evidence that was beyond anything the best fiction writers could come up with about an unhinged, crooked president.

Of course, this won't change the opinions of the outlier MAGA kooks. And Trump's diehard loyalists will no doubt double down and try to discredit her. Considering the support she is getting from former Trump White House staffers, attacking Hutchinson would be a mistake. Not that that would stop them.

But with the new evidence of witness tampering, and with more revelations coming from the committee in the weeks ahead, the eggshell wrapped around Trump's most loyal sycophants might begin to show signs of cracking. Thieves and crooks, to protect themselves, usually turn on each other. And then there's the DOJ.

It looks like Trump's defense is going to be: "Who are you gonna believe, an attractive, intelligent articulate woman privy to conversations among my closest, most ardent loyalists and a few turncoats who testified under oath; or a fact-denying, unhinged pathological liar and a few loyalists who are willing to go down with a sinking ship all of whom have refused to testify under oath." Really a tough choice—but not for sane Americans who believe in the Constitution, democracy and the rule of law.

TO BIG TO JAIL?

In 1974, after Richard Nixon resigned the presidency, his successor, Gerald Ford, issued Nixon a blanket pardon. This prevented Nixon from ever facing criminal charges, a jury of ordinary citizens and the prospects of jail time.

Now, as evidence mounts against Donald Trump, with him no longer president, and with a democrat in the White House, the prospects of a presidential pardon to bail him out is not on the table. But there is a legitimate question that must be considered, especially since Trump faces charges not only at the federal level, but from states as well. Georgia and New York come immediately to mind.

With the scope of possible charges far broader than what Nixon might have faced, the question is: Is Donald Trump too big to jail?

If Trump is to be charged, that will be up to the Department of Justice. If he is charged with seditious conspiracy resulting from the mob attacking the capital, and obstruction of justice in seeking to prevent the orderly transition of power by certifying the Electoral College vote, and perhaps others, then what happens?

Remember that, in Nixon's case, the Supreme Court made it clear when he tried to block access to his White House tapes, that "no man is above the law," not even the president. But back then, Nixon had lost not only in the Supreme Court, but in the Congress where he would have faced certain impeachment and conviction, and in the court of public opinion. All the walls had closed in on him.

Times and circumstances are different now. Despite all of Trump's demonstrated peccadillos and crimes, charging him and forcing him to face real jail time comes with real consequences. First, his diehard supporters and extreme loyalists will no doubt declare the filing of charges as nothing more than a partisan political attack against him.

They will make Trump out to be a victim of the never Trumpers, a line he has been repeating every time pressure is applied to him. They will charge those who charge him with being part of a vast conspiracy to thwart the will of the people, the real patriots here. We've already seen this line of attack in full operation.

Already his supporters are saying the House select committee's hearings are nothing more than a planned, orchestrated show designed to paint Trump in a bad light. Of course, the capital attack was a planned event, and even a jury trial is a planned event involving the orderly selection and presentation of witnesses and evidence, but that doesn't matter to the MAGA crowd hellbent on finding conspiracies wherever their minds take them.

Then there's the matter of the trial judge and jury selection.

It will not be that easy to select a jury without at least one who might believe that all of the actions taken against Trump are so much noise and much ado about nothing. Recall that the Republican National Committee called January 6 just some supporters engaging in "legitimate political discourse." That five law enforcement officers died, and over 140 were injured, is lost on, or means nothing to, the MAGA diehards.

The real prospect of what we saw in the O.J. Simpson trial could well be repeated in a Trump trial: jury nullification. The jury could spend weeks listening to the testimony and simply return a verdict of not guilty in a matter of hours via a jury that effectively nullifies the evidence, testimony and ultimate accountability. For them, something about putting a former president behind bars is anathema; they simply won't allow it.

Then there's the judge. A judge can influence the trial process by his/her handling of the jury selection process, or voir dire; evidentiary rulings, allowing testimony to be received but, more importantly, preventing evidence from ever reaching the jury's eyes and ears; jury instructions, and even whether to let a case go to the jury. There have been criminal trials that have had overbearing judges influencing the outcome. The magnitude of a trial against Trump should be self-evident. So many careers will be made or broken by this. And Trump did appoint more than 200 federal judges at the trial and appellate levels. What are the chances one or more of the judges passing judgment will be a Trump appointee? Of course, many Trump appointees had no difficulty dismissing his "rigged" election lawsuits, but a trial against Trump himself is a completely different dynamic.

Right now, the final decision to charge and prosecute lies with Attorney General Merrick Garland. A former judge, he will make every effort to assure that there is no stone unturned in making this decision. He will decide based on how airtight the case is, how strong and believable the witnesses are, and whether he believes he can get jurors to put aside their personal feelings and render a decision based solely on the evidence presented in court, and the judge's instructions on the law.

The prosecution lawyers will be the best and the brightest; Trump's lawyers will be the best he can obtain. The stakes could not be higher.

Of course, Garland could decide not to prosecute. Such a decision, however, will force further decisions about prosecuting Trump's allies; those who aided and abetted January 6, those who asked for pardons, etc.

And then, there would be outrage among those who believe "no man is above the law" and the rule of law applies equally to everyone. Everyone.

Uneasy lies the head of the Attorney General of the United States. He is the first who will ask himself this question: Is Trump too big to jail?

RACE RIOTS V. AN ATTEMPTED COUP: THERE IS NO COMPARISION

Our nation has a sordid history of race riots. Beginning with 1967, there have been dozens of race riots in hundreds of cities leading to hundreds of deaths and property destruction into the billions. The causes of these riots differ, but all involve claims, in one form or another, of police over aggressiveness and brutality.

Below is a brief description of the major racial conflicts and riots since then. The purpose of this is not to show the expanse of this part of our nation's history. Rather, it's a result of far too many who seek to somehow dismiss or justify the January 6 assault on our nation's capital by comparing the loss of life and property damage on that day to the greater numbers in these many riots. The causative factors demonstrate that there is simply no comparison.

Following the 1967 riots, President Lyndon Johnson appointed a National Advisory Commission on Civil Disorders (the Kerner Commission) to investigate the violent disorders that had erupted in 15 U.S. cities, including Detroit, since 1965. The commission's 1968 report cited white racism, discrimination, and poverty as among the causative factors and famously warned that "our nation is moving toward two societies, one black, one white—separate and unequal."

In the past few years, we learned the names of Freddie Gray, Michael Brown and George Floyd, as well as others. Much of what is in the Kerner Commission report remains valid today, regardless of how many attempts are being made to re-write or ignore our nation's sad history on this subject.

Those riots grew out of grievances over treatment of Blacks by law enforcement, mixed with poverty and a "no way out" mentality.

Now contrast that with January 6. A president of the United States knew that his supporters were armed and were not going to harm him. He was hellbent on stopping the constitutionally mandated certification of the election results and the orderly transition of power. He instigated a riot at the nation's capital to accomplish that singular purpose. People died and many were injured, including law enforcement. This president was aided and abetted by elected and appointed Republican Party officials and cronies, all of whom acted as they did based on a lie pitched repeatedly by this president. To this day, he continues to double down on his Big Lie.

Those who rioted years ago were, to a large extent, fighting for those words that say, "all men are created equal" and" equal justice under law." The inalienable rights "of life, liberty and the pursuit of happiness." When arrested without justification, without probable cause; when assaulted without instigation; when shot and wounded or killed when unarmed and posing no threat, anger builds. When those quoted words fly in the face of the reality in front of them, anger explodes. Violence is not justified, but it is explainable in this light.

What were the rioters fighting for on January 6? To do the bidding of one man and his allies to remain in office unconstitutionally and illegally based not on fact, based not on justice (having lost more than 60 cases), but on a lie bought hook, line and sinker. Unexplainable and unjustifiable.

Rioters fighting for what they perceive as the American Dream vs. rioters fighting to overthrow the government based on a lie that this president knew was a lie.

Trying to equate the two would be laughable if it weren't deadly serious. What makes this feckless attempt at moral equivalency dangerous is that the same line can be used should another wayward president decide to take the law into his own hands and lead another attempted coup if the election results don't go his way.

Of course, the number of deaths and destruction of property caused by the many riots going back in time far exceed that of January 6. But comparing the two for the purpose giving some level of comfort to the insurrectionists, is dangerous and quite nonsensical. The race riots were never about overthrowing the nation's government; it was about being accorded equal treatment under the law. January 6 was about a coup directed by, and to please, one man.

And of course, those rioters were charged with criminal violations, prosecuted and imprisoned. And recently, wayward law enforcement officers have been tried, convicted and sentenced.

How many of those who instigated the insurrection, or egged on the rioters, have been charged and prosecuted to date: None.

In the interest of full disclosure: here is a list of racial conflicts:

Following the assassination of Dr. Martin Luther King in 1968, riots broke out in 128 cities. Government statistics further show the number of racial incidents over the years: 1969 (2), 1970 (4), 1971 (6), 1972(3), 1973 (1). From 1974 to 1989 (9).

Since 1990, the following racial incidences, including riots, occurred:

1990--1996: Wynwood riot (Puerto Ricans rioted after a jury acquitted six officers accused of beating a Puerto Rican drug dealer to death); 1991: Overtown, Miami – In the heavily Black section against Cuban Americans, like earlier riots which occurred there in 1982 and 1984; 1991 Washington, D.C. riot – Riots following the shooting of a Salvadoran man by a police officer in the Mount Pleasant neighborhood, aggravated by grievances which were felt by Latinos in the district; 1992 Los Angeles riots – April 29 to May 4 – a series of riots, lootings, arsons and civil disturbance that occurred in Los Angeles County, California in 1992, following the acquittal of police officers on trial regarding the assault of Rodney King; 1996: St. Petersburg, Florida riot of 1996, caused by protests against racial profiling and police brutality.

2001-2012: 2001 Cincinnati riots – April – in the African-American section of Over-the-Rhine; 2009: Oakland, CA – Riots following the BART Police shooting of Oscar Grant; 2012: Anaheim, California Riot—followed the shooting of two Hispanic males

2015-2021: 2015 Baltimore riots – Riots following the death of Freddie Gray; 2015: Ferguson unrest – Riots following the anniversary of the shooting of Michael Brown; 2016 Milwaukee riots – Riots following the fatal shooting of 23 year old Sylville Smith;2016: Charlotte riot, September

20–21 – Riots started in response to the shooting of Keith Lamont Scott by police; 2017: Assault of DeAndre Harris, August 12 – Far-right extremists cause the assault of DeAndre Harris during the Unite the Right rally in Charlottesville, Virginia; 2020–2021 United States racial unrest – Ongoing protests sparked by the murder of George Floyd, numerous disturbances broke out in other cities.

MY LIST OF "160+" GREATEST VOCALS OF THE ROCK ERA

I am a creature of lists. I want to know the 10 greatest of this; the 100 best of that—you get the idea. I doubt I'm alone in searching lists. I am also a product of the music of the 50s and 60s. I doubt I'm alone here either, although there is an age factor involved in favoring this musical genre.

Recently, I decided to create a playlist on my Alexa that consists of what in my view are the top vocals of the rock era. I searched my memory and came up with about 100. Then I went to Google and came up with 164.

I mentioned what I had done to a friend, who suggested I might want to share it in case others might like to do the same. So, here is my list of what I consider the greatest vocals of the rock era—with emphasis on the 1950s through the 1960s--in no particular order. I hope my list brings back memories, and if you decide to create your own playlist, I hope you enjoy your walk down memory lane as much as I do.

Treat Me Nice	Elvis Presley
Too Much	Elvis Presley
Hard-Headed Woman	Elvis Presley
It's Only Make-Believe	Conway Twitty
El Paso	Marty Robbins
I Can't Stop Loving You	Ray Charles
Walk Right In	Rooftop Singers
Deep Purple	Nino Tempo/April Stevens
Everybody Loves Somebody	Dean Martin
Baby Love	Supremes
You've Lost that Loving Feeling	Righteous Brothers
Help Me Rhonda	Beach Boys
Alone at Last	Jackie Wilson
Love Me	Elvis Presley
Maybe	Chantels
Happy Happy Birthday Baby	Tune Weavers
Love Me With all your Heart	Engelbert Humperdinck
Monday, Monday	Mamas and Papas
I Can't Help Myself	Four Tops
Good Vibrations	Beach Boys
To Sir with Love	Lulu
Night	Jackie Wilson
Istanbul	Four Lads
I Heard it through the Grapevine	Marvin Gaye
Hey Jude	The Beatles
Heartache Tonight	Eagles
Get Back	Beatles
Everything is Beautiful	Ray Stevens
Philadelphia Freedom	Elton John
Bad Blood	Neil Sedaka
Dancing Queen	ABBA
Southern Nights	Glen Campbell
You Light Up My Life	Debbie Boone
Alone	Heart
I Still Haven't Found What I'm Looking For	U2
Roll With It	Steve Winwood
Kokomo	Beach Boys
Black Velvet	Alannah Myles
Vision of Love	Mariah Carey
Things	Bobby Darin
Believe	Cher

Cara Mia	Jay and the Americans
Only You	Platters
Magic Touch	Platters
Kewpie Doll	Perry Como
Glendora	Perry Como
Crying	Roy Orbison
Let the Four Winds Blow	Fats Domino
Laughter in the Rain	Neil Sedaka
No Other Love	Perry Como
Mean Woman Blues	Roy Orbison
Wonderful, Wonderful	Johnny Mathis
You are my Destiny	Paul Anka
Footsteps	Steve Lawrence
Waterloo	ABBA
Naughty Lady of Shady Lane	Ames Brothers
Baker Street	Gerry Rafferty
Margaritaville	Jimmy Buffett
Bad Moon Rising	Credence Clearwater Revival
Burnin' Love	Elvis Presley
On the Street Where you Live	Vic Damone
Dream Lover	Bobby Darin
Come Go with Me	Del Vikings
The Stroll	The Diamonds
Ruby Baby	Dion
Save the Last Dance for Me	Drifters
Hold Me	Fleetwood Mac
Many Tears Ago	Connie Francis
Don't it Make my Brown Eyes Blue	Crystal Gayle
Wayward Wind	Gogi Grant
Photographs	Ringo Starr
I Remember You	Frank Ifield
My Sweet Lord	George Harrison
Sad Songs	Elton John
She's a Lady	Tom Jones
Pretty Little Angel Eyes	Curtis Lee
I Love You Always Forever	Donna Lewis
The Heart of Rock and Roll	Huey Lewis and the News
Footloose	Kenny Loggins
Cry Me a River	Julie London
Did You Ever Have to Make up Your Mind	Lovin' Spoonful
Words of Love	Mamas and Papas

I Write the Songs	Barry Manilow
Dancing in the Street	Martha and the Vandellas
My Love	Paul McCartney
A Lover's Question	Clyde McPhatter
Nights in White Satin	Moody Blues
I Got a Feeling	Rickey Nelson
In The Still of the Night	Five Satins
In Dreams	Roy Orbison
How High the Moon	Les Paul and Mary Ford
To Know Him is to Love Him	Teddy Bears
Young Girl	Gary Puckett/Union Gap
Crazy Little Thing Called Love	Queen
Mountain of Love	Johnny Rivers
Don't Worry	Marty Robbins
Since I Don't Have You	Skyliners
What in the World's Come Over You?	Jack Scott
I Just Can't Help Believin'	B. J. Thomas
Broken Hearted Melody	Sarah Vaughn
Sir Duke	Stevie Wonder
You're the One	The Vogues
Lover Please	Clyde McPhatter
Hey Baby	Bruce Channel
Achy Breaky Heart	Billy Ray Cyrus
All By Myself	Eric Carmen
Am I That Easy to Forget	Engelbert Humperdinck
Baby The Rain Must Fall	Glenn Yarbrough
Believe What You Say	Rickey Nelson
Blue Blue Day	Don Gibson
Born Too Late	Poni-Tails
Blue	LeAnn Rimes
Bristol Stomp	The Dovells
But I Do	Clarence Henry
Clementine	Bobby Darin
Could This Be Magic	Dubs
Cradle of Love	Johnny Preston
Don't Let the Sun Go Down on Me	Elton John
Don't Stop	Fleetwood Mac
Dream Lover	Bobby Darin
Dream On Little Dreamer	Perry Como
Early in the Morning	Rinky Dinks
Feel So Fine	Johnny Preston

Fernando	ABBA
Five O'Clock World	The Vogues
Gone	Ferlin Husky
House of the Rising Sun	Animals
I Can Hear Music	Beach Boys
I Will	Dean Martin
I'll Be Satisfied	Jackie Wilson
Lucky Old Sun	Frankie Laine
Jingle Bell Rock	Bobby Helms
Just Born	Perry Como
Lady Madonna	Beatles
Lady Willpower	Gary Puckett
Lion Sleeps Tonight	Tokens
One Summer Night	Danleers
Pretty Blue Eyes	Steve Lawrence
She's Not You	Elvis Presley
Spanish Eyes	Al Martino
Stoned Love	Supremes
Such a Night	Elvis Presley
Tallahassee Lassie	Freddie Cannon
That's Where the Music Takes Me	Neil Sedaka
To Be Loved	Jackie Wilson
Way Down	Elvis Presley
Wonder of You	Elvis Presley
You	Monotones
You're the One	The Vogues
Your Love Keeps Lifting Me Higher	Jackie Wilson
One Fine Day	Chiffons
Slippin and Sliden	Little Richard
Something To Talk About	Bonnie Raitt
Take a Chance on Me	ABBA
Tears of A Clown	Miracles
TROUBLE	Elvis Presley
Something About the Way You Look Tonight	Elton John
Club at the End of the Steet	Elton John
Only You	Platters
Cry	Johnnie Ray
Come Running Back	Dean Martin
Houston	Dean Martin
You've Lost That Lovin' Feeling	Righteous Brothers
I've Had The Time of my Life	Medley/Warnes

PRIVACY RIGHTS, SECOND AMENDMENT AND HONESTY IN CONSTITUTIONAL INTERPRETATION

Whether there is a federal constitutional right to choose to have an abortion or not, depends on how the Constitution is to be interpreted. To be sure, the word "abortion" does not appear in the Constitution; neither do words such as "interstate rail system," "airplanes," "nuclear weapons," etc., yet Congress is free to regulate on these, and many other subjects even in the absence of any reference to them.

The six conservative Supreme Court justices who recently overruled the constitutional right of abortion declared that there is nothing in the Constitution that references abortion, and it's not a liberty interest that deserves federal constitutional protection. They take an originalist approach to constitutional interpretation, discerning the intent of the charter's framers at the time of adoption in 1788, and the text of the Constitution itself.

The Constitution also is silent on the word "privacy." Will the Court's conservative majority overrule all cases founded on such a right?

Time will tell.

The other school of constitutional interpretation, the "living constitutionalists," discern a right of privacy from six amendments:

The First Amendment involves the right of to freely practice one's religion, speak one's mind, gather and report the news, assemble together and petition for redress of grievances. These are all personal rights granted to each of us as individuals.

The Third Amendment prohibits a soldier from being quartered in any home during time of peace without the owner's consent, thus recognizing an individual's zone of privacy within his home.

The Fourth Amendment recognizes the right of the people to be secure in their persons, houses, papers, and effects, against unreasonable searches and seizures, except upon probable cause and with a clear description of what is to be searched. Protected by this amendment are privacy rights to your person (or body), your home, papers and other items that constitute your personal effects. Again, here is another constitutional description of personal, private individual rights.

The Fifth Amendment prohibits the government from compelling any individual in any criminal case to be a witness against himself, nor be deprived of life, liberty, or property, without due process of law. This is the individual right to remain silent, your thoughts are private.

The Ninth Amendment recognizes that the rights set out in in the Constitution are not exclusive, and those rights shall not be construed to deny or disparage others retained by the people. What are these other rights not in the Constitution?

What are these additional rights retained by the people? The point here is that the Constitution is not the creator of all personal, individual rights that are guaranteed to the people—us.

Finally, the Fourteenth Amendment prohibits the states from depriving any person of life, liberty, or property, without due process of law; nor deny to any person within its jurisdiction the equal protection of the laws.

Note that the word "liberty" appears in both the Fifth and Fourteenth Amendments. What does liberty mean? As used in Constitution, liberty means freedom from arbitrary and unreasonable restraint upon an individual. Freedom from restraint refers to more than just physical restraint, but also the freedom to act according to one's own will.

Note the last few words: "Freedom to act according to one's own will." If it is a woman's "own will" to have an abortion under reasonable regulations, isn't her constitutionally guaranteed right liberty impacted adversely? Of course it is, but that doesn't stop the originalists and anti-abortionists from carrying the day. By 6-3.

Originalists rail that the privacy rights found in Griswold (contraceptives) Roe (abortion) and same sex marriage (Obergefell) were created out of thin air, as if by magic. In cavalierly dismissing these cases, they do a great disservice by their disingenuousness. Rather than taking this simplistic approach, it would far better serve their interests if they at least tacitly recognized that there are six constitutional amendments that address personal, individual rights of a privacy nature that government cannot intrude upon. To say that privacy rights are a creature of whole cloth is understandable coming from originalists, but it's bogus as the texts of these amendments demonstrate.

Of course, flipping the script, originalists had no difficulty creating an individual right to keep and bear arms, despite the clear prefatory language of the Second Amendment. Recall this amendment provides: "A well regulated Militia, being necessary to the security of a free State, the right of the people to keep and bear Arms, shall not be infringed." Art. I, Sec. 8 of the Constitution authorizes Congress "To provide for organizing, arming, and disciplining, the Militia, and for governing such Part of them as may be employed in the Service of the United States, reserving to the States respectively, the Appointment of the Officers, and the Authority of training the Militia according to the discipline prescribed by Congress…"

Nothing here establishes a personal right to keep and bear arms; the use of the word "militia" is quite instructive of that. It is entirely up to Congress to set the parameters of the "militia," and provide for its right to keep and bear arms. But this didn't stop the conservative originalists from doing for the Second Amendment what they accuse the living constitutionalists of doing for these six amendments to "create" a right of privacy and its several manifestations.

I suppose the Constitution means whatever is in the eye of the beholder, so long as there is a majority of five on the Supreme Court.

WHAT DO WE REALLY THINK?

We are witnessing a rather strange phenomenon, where those on the left and right politically believe the other side is moronic and non-thinkers, while engaging in self-praise for being the real thinkers in America.

Both sides agree the nation is headed in the "wrong direction," without clearly setting out what is the "right direction." So, perhaps it is important to try to discern what both sides actually think today.

It's impossible to cover the waterfront in a deliberately short narrative, and historians will have a field day describing America in the second and third decades of the 21st century. But here is an encapsulation of current major points.

What does the right wing think? Here are a few obvious points:

1. The overriding force driving the right wing is that government is not the solver of problems; it's the cause of the problems.
2. Donald Trump lost because the election was rigged against him.

3. Those who attacked the capital were actually members of the BLM and Antifa dressed up as Trump supporters. As a backup, those rioters were merely engaging in "legitimate political discourse."
4. Any investigation of Trump and his allies is a witch hunt, a hatchet job or a hoax.
5. The Republicans are the party of less taxes, limited government and the rule of law.
6. The left has been historically wrong, and the conservative movement has consistently been correct.

The right's chief deep thinkers in government are Sens. Ted Cruz, Josh Hawley, Rand Paul, John Kennedy (not the former president), Tom Cotton, Lindsey Graham, etc., and Reps. Jim Jordan, Marjorie Taylor Greene, Lauren Boebert, Matt Gaetz, Mo Brooks, Paul Gosar, etc. and Governors Greg Abbott, Ron DeSantis and Doug Ducey, etc. They have distinguished themselves among our intellectual elite by: promoting conspiracy theories, favoring white nationalists, re-writing history, trashing academic freedom via thought control policing, enacting suppressive voting laws designed to cut into opposition voting, etc.

Lots of deep thinking here.

What does the left wing think? Here are a few obvious points:

1. Government is not the problem; it's the conservatives' business-driven policies that have been the problem.

2. BLM and Antifa protest police brutality and a history of unequal treatment under the law. Donald Trump's supporters backed his Big Lie.
3. Donald Trump lost because he got fewer votes nationally and in the Electoral College.
4. Those who attacked the capital were not BLM or Antifa; they were Trump supporters egged on by Trump himself, knowing the mob was armed, not gunning for him, but gunning for his vice president.
5. The investigations of Trump and his cronies are legitimately being conducted by both federal and state officials. It is Republicans who have stonewalled, avoided subpoenas, plead the Fifth Amendment and sought pardons—not acts of innocent people.
6. Sen. Rick Scott of Florida is exhibit A in showing that the Republicans want to raise taxes of the more vulnerable. Two presidents who raised the national debt significantly were Ronald Reagan and Donald Trump. Those who attacked the capital that led to the death of five officers and injuries to more than 140 were mad insurrectionists seeking to overthrow the government—hardly the stuff of law and order and the rule of law.

Some deep thinking going on here.

The conservatives were historically wrong to let the private sector run amuck in the 1920s, and Republican policies drove the nation's economy over the cliff, leading to the Great Depression in 1929. The conservatives were wrong in appeasing Hitler in the late 1930s, which allowed him and his allies to gain strength and wage war. It was only after Franklin Roosevelt's New Deal and wartime policies took center stage that we were able to overcome both Republican Party failings. Further, the conservatives were wrong on civil rights, voting rights and other issues that favored the vast majority of Americans. Their policies favored—and continue to favor—an

America of the pre- and post-Civil War time, particularly in the south; policies driven by race and religion.

Every one of the right wing's six points above has been debunked by facts, whether the fact-deniers like it or not. To be sure, the left has had its share of failings, but on the Richter Scale of blunders, there is no comparison.

This isn't my opinion; check the history books. You know, the ones the right wing is trying to censor or re-write.

THE FAR-RIGHT WING'S VERSION OF AMERICA

Government policies premised on Evangelical Christian religion.

Guns of all makes and styles, concealed and open carry, proliferating on the streets, roadways, in schools, churches, malls, movie theaters, etc.

White nationalists and neo-Nazis proudly marching on our nation's streets and roadways, supported and cheered on by public officeholders and officials who tell them they're loved and are true patriots.

Women banned from making decisions about their own well-being.

Right wing state legislators determining the outcome of presidential elections regardless of the state vote totals.

Voter access to the polls tamped down by supposedly neutral-appearing laws, but in reality, targeting historic group voting patterns to suppress turnout.

American history and civics re-written, designed to indoctrinate and glorify a false narrative, rather than educate so people will learn from history's blunders and tragedies.

University and college curriculum sanitized to eliminate any questioning of right-wing authority; indoctrination under the guise, and in the name of, academic freedom.

Laws stifling the executive branch of the federal government from taking contemporaneous measures to address serious national crises like global warming, resulting in greater harm to the environment, and our overall well-being.

(You don't think a national religion is in the grand scheme of things? Here is Colorado Rep. Lauren Boebert's speech before a church group: "The reason we had so many overreaching regulations in our nation is because the church complied. The Church is supposed to direct the government. That is not how our Founding Fathers intended it. And I'm tired of this separation of church and state junk. That's not in the Constitution." She's absolutely wrong on this, but to her audience, and those who agree with her, being wrong doesn't matter.

These are some of the pages in the right-wing playbook for the takeover of our democratic form of government. Of course, they claim they support true democracy—just the way Hitler and other totalitarians claimed they were advancing nationalism, law and order and freedom. Fortunately, we know from history how that turned out, but the history revisionists have this in their line of sight.

George Orwell was most prescient when he said "Who controls the past controls the future. Who controls the present controls the past."

To gain control of the future, first must come control of the past. And those who control the present control the past. This is precisely why the extreme right wing is so fixated on using its admittedly minority strength in key places today to control the present by the actions described above. By controlling the present, they can work to control the past by re-writing it, to the point of denying some of our history, while overhyping others, resulting in a false, even dangerous, narrative—the danger being that if the perils and pitfalls of history are not known, they are repeated, with disastrous consequences.

History teaches that when the legislative and executive branches of government are co-opted by an ideology, people turn to the courts. But what happens if the judiciary is similarly co-opted? Where do people go to redress their grievances?

This is not the time for silence or acquiescence. The almost 250-year grand experiment in self-governing is on the line.

THEY HAVE IT ALL PLANNED FOR US

In the world of fiction, the right-wing extremists have it all planned out for us. As smart and sure of themselves as they believe they are, and as confident and smug in their belief that they know what is best for all of us, they are determined to make the rest of us go along with their plans.

If they have their way, they will tell us:

What to know and what not to know.

What to believe and what not to believe.

What we can learn and what we can't learn.

What we can read and what we can't read.

What we can say and what we can't say.

What we can think and what we can't think.

What can be taught and what can't be taught.

What we can write and what we can't write.

Who we can criticize and who is beyond criticism.

What must be accepted and what must be rejected.

How we are live.

How we are to act.

How we are to think.

What we are to say.

What we are to do.

All of this will be neatly packaged in freedom, liberty and justice. It will be wrapped in the rule of law and the American Flag.

And everybody will be happy. As long as everyone does precisely as told. Questions will not be tolerated, for that leads to uncomfortable feelings. Resistance will be punished; and we can't have dissent in this brave new world. Everyone must get along and be happy.

Remember the phrase "live and let live," that we should tolerate the opinions and behavior of others so that they will similarly tolerate your own. It's being replaced by "we will tell you how to live, and you will live by what we tell you."

This is all the product of those deep thinkers, the bastion of the supreme intelligence of the extreme far right. We've seen their brilliance on full display, particularly over the past few years. We saw it when the Trump rioters stormed the capital on January 6. We saw it when his supporters marched under the banners of Proud Boys and Oath Keepers in Charlottesville, Idaho and Michigan, among other places.

We see their intellectual brilliance in the halls of Congress with the likes of Sens. Ted Cruz, Josh Hawley, Rand Paul, John Kennedy (not the former president), Tom Cotton, Lindsey Graham, etc., and Reps. Jim Jordan, Marjorie Taylor Greene, Lauren Boebert, Matt Gaetz, Mo Brooks, Paul Gosar, etc. and Governors Greg Abbott, Ron DeSantis and Doug Ducey, etc. They have distinguished themselves among our intellectual elite by: promoting conspiracy theories, favoring white nationalists, re-writing history, trashing academic freedom via thought control policing, enacting suppressive voting laws designed to cut into opposition voting, etc. If they can make law that makes illegal legal, or makes legal illegal, then so be it.

We see this shining example of immense brain power at MAGA rallies where Trump's supporters show their undying love for a pathological liar who is facing serious criminal charges involving seditious conduct and obstruction of justice, and perhaps many others.

Real smart folks here.

To be sure, the core five extreme conservatives on the Supreme Court are doing the bidding of these officials, their allies and supporters. Not content with overturning a 50-year constitutional right—the first time the Court has ever overruled a constitutional right--and assaulting the bedrock separation of church and state in favor of a move toward a theocracy where "the church directs the government," in the words of Rep. Boebert, the far-right justices are now poised to attack the very foundation of our Democracy, the right to vote.

The Supreme Court will hear a case from North Carolina that could radically reshape how federal elections are conducted by giving state legislatures independent power, not subject to review by state courts, to set election rules in conflict with state constitutions. Republicans call it the independent state legislature doctrine; the underpinning of this case could open the door to state legislatures sending their own slates of presidential electors, trashing the will of the voters in favor of the sole, state court unreviewable decision of state legislatures. Historically, elections have been conducted by the states; this would change dramatically and draconianly.

According to conservative former federal appeals Judge J. Michael Luttig, "The independent state legislature doctrine says that, under the Elections and the Electors Clauses of the Constitution, state legislatures possess plenary and exclusive power over the conduct of federal presidential elections and the selection of state presidential electors. Not even a state supreme court, let alone other state elections officials, can alter the legislatively written election rules or interfere with the appointment of state electors by the legislatures, under this theory."

The doctrine is based on a reading of two similar provisions of the U.S. Constitution. The one at issue in the North Carolina case, the Elections Clause, says: "The times, places and manner of holding elections for senators and representatives, shall be prescribed in each state by the legislature thereof."

That means, North Carolina Republicans argued, that the state legislature has sole responsibility among state institutions for drawing congressional districts and that state courts have no role to play.

The North Carolina Supreme Court rejected the argument that it was not entitled to review the actions of the state legislature, saying that would be "repugnant to the sovereignty of states, the authority of state constitutions and the independence of state courts, and would produce absurd and dangerous consequences."

Pundits have chimed in that this case has the potential to affect many aspects of the 2024 election, including by giving the justices power to influence the presidential race if disputes arise over how state courts interpret state election laws.

In taking up the case, the court could upend nearly every facet of the American electoral process, allowing state legislatures to set new rules, regulations and districts on federal elections with few checks against overreach, and potentially create a chaotic system with differing rules and voting eligibility for presidential elections.

In short, state legislatures would have the power to reject the state's vote totals and replace them with the will of the elected legislators. The effect of such a decision by the conservative majority would destroy the fundamental individual right to vote set out in several amendments to the Constitution.

Currently, Republicans have complete control over 30 state legislatures, according to the National Conference of State Legislatures, and were the force behind a wave of new voting restrictions passed last year. And Republican legislatures in key battleground states like Wisconsin, Pennsylvania and North Carolina have used their control over redistricting to effectively lock in power for a decade. Democrats control 17 state legislatures.

But as we celebrate our Independence Day, a Court that is steeped in protecting settled precedent and avoiding judicial activism would not dare to set aside the fundamental right to vote, would it? Would it?

Of course, this is all fiction, right? Right?

CALIFORNIA DEMOCRAT GOV. GAVIN NEWSOM IN 2024?

I have long believed Newsom would make a strong candidate for president. He couldn't have won in 2020, but 2024 has a different set of dynamics in play. Of course, the Republican Party will cast him as a flaming left-wing extremist wanting to take away freedom and liberty, couched in "your rights," but the party loyalists would make that claim against anyone to the left of Marjorie Taylor Greene and her cohorts, so there's nothing new there.

Moreover, sooner or later, the same party line repeated ad nauseam tends to become hollow. And the republicans certainly have their own problems with a former president fixated on redemption and vengeance, but facing serious criminal charges stemming a large part from testimony and evidence provided by Republican officials and operatives. You can bet the Democrats will hang Trump's considerable baggage on the party's nominees.

If Trump implodes, DeSantis becomes the prime prospect, but he'll be cast as Trump with less baggage, and just as ideological and authoritarian. As for the Democrats, Biden ran as the only one who could beat Trump, and he did--no matter what Trump and his blind loyalists think or say. But age is a major factor, and he's having difficulty forging a message that resonates with the electorate. His VP hasn't exactly electrified the party's faithful, and it may well come time for the party to look elsewhere. California is vote rich on both popular and Electoral College fronts.

If there are other democrat candidates out there who have the base Newsom has, and the platform he has, I haven't seen evidence of it. Another factor is that he is media-savvy, and is not afraid to put the Republicans on the defensive by accusing them of being extremists hellbent on taking away rights.

His list of grievances against the party and its compliant Supreme Court conservative bloc will certainly arouse the party's base; no one else seems to be doing that. Newsom has already beaten back Republican efforts to oust him, and the failed recall effort has in fact strengthened his hand, He is expected to cruise toward re-election; DeSantis, on the other hand, might not get that great vote he expects. Makes for interesting times going forward.

GOVERNMENT'S GREATEST RESPONSIBILITY: KEEPING US SAFE

There is no doubt that the greatest responsibility of government is to protect its citizens from violence. Providing for the public health and welfare of the citizens is of less importance if there is a credible threat of violence at any time.

As one historian noted, "The idea of government as protector requires taxes to fund, train and equip an army and a police force; to build courts and jails; and to elect or appoint the officials to pass and implement the laws citizens must not break. Regarding foreign threats, government as protector requires the ability to meet and treat with other governments as well as to fight them. This minimalist view of government is clearly on display in the early days of the American Republic, comprised of the President, Congress, Supreme Court, and departments of Treasury, War, State and Justice."

But as statistics mount, the job of government officials has become more difficult and, sadly in some cases, they have failed at this their greatest duty.

Since the mass shooting at Columbine High School in 1999 that claimed the lives of 15 students and one faculty member, including the two shooters, there have been an additional 229 U.S. school shootings. That's 10 a year, or almost one a month.

In the past 23 years, more than 311,000 students have experienced gun violence in our nation's schools.

This doesn't include shootings in malls, movie theaters, churches, shopping centers, and other places where the public congregates.

After the July 4 mass shooting at an Independence Day parade in Illinois, we can add parades to the list of places where mass shootings can occur.

Since 2017 and including this latest horrific incident, there have been 96 mass shootings across the country. That's 19 per year, or one every five to six weeks.

Many of us can remember going to a place of public gatherings and not give a thought to the horrible possibility of facing a mass shooting event. Tragically, this is not the case anymore.

Some will no doubt argue that, considering the size of the country and the number of public places available, the statistics are not really out of the ordinary. This argument is based on the belief that these incidents are going to occur, and there is nothing that can be done about it. In a rather sordid way, this is the "it's just the way life is now" argument.

There are also repeated references to the mental health of the perpetrator, as if more must be done to weed out those who might pose a threat of a real and present nature.

Unfortunately, we never really know when someone is going to snap, and a person may have no record of violence until some grudge or moment of anger sets him off on a rampage. Moreover, studies by mental health experts debunk the notion that most mass shootings are committed by the mentally ill. Further studies show that domestic terrorism by right-wing extremists is on the rise. According to the Anti-Defamation League, since 2010, right-wing extremists have been responsible for 330 deaths, or 76 percent of all domestic extremist-related murders within that time.

There are those who believe increasing the presence of law enforcement will deter these crimes of mass murder. Tell that to the parents and families in Uvalde, Texas, as their loved ones were gunned down while police stood idly by, more concerned with protecting the officers than the students and faculty.

There are deft excuses that are supposed to give some sort of comfort in defense of doing little or nothing, but they don't mask the reality of what they really are: just excuses.

The point of this is not to cast blame; that serves no purpose and won't bring back the victims or give peace of mind to their families and friends.

The point is that we have a mass shooting epidemic, and those responsible for our safety are not doing their job to prevent it. And there is sufficient data to identify the scope of the problem and what needs to be done to deal with it.

The rapidly growing trend of weapons proliferation cuts against dealing with this epidemic. There are simply too many guns in too many hands. We are the only nation where the number of guns in circulation is greater than the total population. Considering the population of those 18 and under, we have an adult population that averages more than two guns per person. To those who argue this degree of weaponization is necessary for self-defense, the reality is that less than two percent of all uses of firearms is for self-defense.

And with the move afoot to allow both concealed and open carry of weapons in public places, it doesn't take any real stretch of the imagination to visualize a dispute in a department store, at a lunch counter, in a parking lot, etc., rapidly turning deadly.

Fear is debilitating. It can paralyze. But no one should fear sending their kids to school, or going to a mall, church, grocery shopping, or even a parade.

If we don't address this national crisis with profound force, if we rely on tepid, feel-good responses that really solve nothing, then fear will become the reality. The effect of this on a free and mobile society should be most clearly evident.

We elect officials to keep us safe. It's time for all of them to do their jobs instead of pandering to those who believe these horrific crimes can't happen to them. They could well be next.

INTERESTING DATA ON GUNS

Nearly half of republicans believe America has to live with mass shootings. A recent poll shows 44 percent of Republicans believe mass shootings are the price we must pay to live in a free society. This same CBS/YouGov poll shows 62% support for a nationwide ban on semi-automatic rifles

Studies by mental health experts debunk the notion that most mass shootings are committed by the mentally ill. They simply are not. The simple fact is most mass shooters are terrorists, not mentally ill.

Further studies show that domestic terrorism by right-wing extremists is on the rise. According to the Anti-Defamation League, since 2010, right-wing extremists have been responsible for 330 deaths, or 76 percent of all domestic extremist-related murders within that time. This debunks the notion that left-wing extremism is primarily responsible for mass shootings.

Finally, the notion that guns are needed for self-defense is also debunked. Statistics show that less than two percent of all uses of firearms involve self-defense.

I wonder if these stoic republicans would have the same view if these mass shootings occurred at schools where their children attended; churches they and their families and friends attended, shopping centers and malls they frequented; movie theaters they attended, etc. It's always easier when it's the others who are being harmed.

CONGRESSMAN KINZINGER INVESTIGATING JANUARY 6 SHARES THREATS AGAINST HIM AND HIS FAMILY

This is clear evidence of a profound crisis in America. It is a crisis of hatred, in this instance directed toward those charged by law with investigating certain actions committed against our government, actions that may well constitute crimes.

Rep. Adam Kinzinger is charged with investigating the conduct of a former president and his cronies in connection with an attack on the nation's capital. There is no mistake about it; he is doing his job, the job he was elected to do. For doing his job, he--and others who are doing theirs--are subject to the most vile and vicious threats for daring to unearth the truth behind the criminal assault on the great symbol of our Democracy.

Sadly, there are those who believe that we are not a nation of laws, but a nation of men. They have been radicalized to believe that certain self-proclaimed patriots are allowed to take the law into their own hands, break the laws duly and legally enacted by government, and be immunized from accountability. The danger to our nation should this ever become the rule of law should be so obvious as to require no discussion.

We simply can't go down this road. This type of vile, vicious hatred is a cancer that will consume both victim and perpetrator. It will eat away at the very fabric of our society. There is no room in our country for this kind of behavior. It should--must--be roundly condemned by those who value our grand experiment in self-government. Sadly, there will be those who greet this latest diatribe with silence, or worse.

If this continues unabated, we will not need to worry about Russia or China. We will destroy ourselves from within.

ANOTHER NUT WITH WEAPONS OF WAR

From the information gathered since the July 4 mass shooting in Illinois, we learned that the shooter is crazy, yet he was able to legally purchase several weapons including assault rifles.

We also learned he had a disturbing paper trail of threats of violence.

With more firearms than people in America, it is certainly reasonable to presume there had to be others who were armed at this parade.

As we've seen in the past, none of this mattered. It didn't matter that this guy was revealing his craziness openly and brazenly. It didn't matter that others at the parade were armed. It didn't matter that with his background, he was legally able to buy weapons of war, and use them on the public streets of an American city.

He is not the first to fit this profile; he won't be the last.

A significant number of republicans simply say "well, this is the price we must pay to live in a free society." We've been a free society for a long time; I don't remember this spate of mass shootings as part of our long history; actually, it has become part of our recent history after a ban on these weapons of war was lifted. But, of course, those who share this stoic and myopic view won't—or don't want to--make that connection.

On January 6, 1941, President Franklin Roosevelt delivered his famous "Four Freedoms" speech. One of the freedoms he addressed was the "freedom from fear." FDR said: "The fourth is freedom from fear, which, translated into world terms, means a world-wide reduction of armaments to such a point and in such a thorough fashion that no nation will be in a position to commit an act of physical aggression against any neighbor—anywhere in the world."

FDR's Four Freedoms formed an important pillar of the Universal Declaration of Human Rights that were adopted on December 10, 1948, by the United Nations General Assembly. The freedom from fear is mentioned in the preamble of the Declaration.

With the increasing number of mass murders that are taking places on our streets, in our schools, churches, shopping malls, movie theaters, etc., his words are most relevant today. With each mass murder, we become less free. We become more afraid. Holiday parades are part of our culture. How many millions who are planning on going to these parades will consider, even for a moment, about mass shootings, and hesitate? When parents send their kids off to school, or go to church, or visit a mall, or go shopping, will there be some consideration, even for the slightest moment, about mass shootings, and send a chill down the spine? There are few things worse than the paralysis of fear; it immobilizes and prevents us from enjoying our freedoms.

These shootings are becoming a part of the American conscience, and that's not freedom from fear.

In 1994, Congress passed, and President Clinton signed a ban on assault weapons. A major study undertaken by The Connection revealed the following:

"From 1981 – the earliest year in our analysis – to the rollout of the assault weapons ban in 1994, the proportion of deaths in mass shootings in which an assault rifle was used was lower than it is today.

Yet in this earlier period, mass shooting deaths were steadily rising. Indeed, high-profile mass shootings involving assault rifles – such as the killing of five children in Stockton, California, in 1989 and a 1993 San Francisco office attack that left eight victims dead – provided the impetus behind a push for a prohibition on some types of gun.

During the 1994-2004 ban: In the years after the assault weapons ban went into effect, the number of deaths from mass shootings fell, and the increase in the annual number of incidents slowed down. Even including 1999's Columbine High School massacre – the deadliest mass shooting during the period of the ban – the 1994 to 2004 period saw lower average annual rates of both mass shootings and deaths resulting from such incidents than before the ban's inception.

From 2004 onward: The data shows an almost immediate – and steep – rise in mass shooting deaths in the years after the assault weapons ban expired in 2004.

Breaking the data into absolute numbers, between 2004 and 2017 – the last year of our analysis – the average number of yearly deaths attributed to mass shootings was 25, compared with 5.3 during the 10-year tenure of the ban and 7.2 in the years leading up to the prohibition on assault weapons.

Saving hundreds of lives

We calculated that the risk of a person in the U.S. dying in a mass shooting was 70% lower during the period in which the assault weapons ban was active. The proportion of overall gun homicides resulting from mass shootings was also down, with nine fewer mass-shooting-related fatalities per 10,000 shooting deaths."

This study ended in 2017. Since then, and including this latest horrific incident, there have been 96 mass shootings across the country. That's 19 per year, or one every five to six weeks. In the past five years, we've seen more rage, more anger, more hatred spill onto our streets and into our communities. Is there a connection between this and the spate of mass murders? This looks like an area for our criminal justice statisticians.

Many of us can remember going to a place of public gatherings and not give a thought to the horrible possibility of facing a mass shooting event. Tragically, this is not the case anymore.

This is not opinion; this is fact. It doesn't square with the opinions of those who would throw up their hands and say nothing can be done to stop this epidemic of violence. In fact, they won't even allow for that chance to be taken.

A ban on assault weapons would have done one thing: it would have made this single nut's chances of getting his hands on those war weapons that much harder, if not impossible. And it might well have worked to prevent others similarly profiled in the past, and might well prevent future similarly profiled perpetrators from carrying out their madness on the innocent.

And that alone might well have saved lives. Isn't a ban on these horrific weapons worth the real prospect of saving lives of children, mothers, fathers, grandmothers, grandfathers, churchgoers, shoppers, and on and on?

Why is there this government paralysis against banning these weapons of war? What great societal benefit do they provide? They aren't used for self-defense. They don't make us safer. They're not part of some plot to take away one's guns—the Second Amendment prevents that. So, what is it that causes those to turn their heads when asked why these weapons of mass destruction remain available for sale, to be used for WHAT?

SEN. LINDSEY GRAHAM REFUSES TO TESTIFY UNDER OATH

This comes as no surprise. Lindsey Graham is a loudmouthed southern politician who believes he's above the law. The so-called "law and order" Republican is being asked to provide important, relevant information to a Georgia grand jury about the 2020 election. He has been informed he is not a subject of the investigation. For someone who is supposed to represent the epitome of what law and order is about, that's obviously not enough. Testifying under oath, where he must tell the truth upon risk of perjury, is frightening for him. He can't spin his BS and babble on about those evil radical left-wing liberals.

Testifying truthfully under oath? Why how un-American is that to ask of a sitting senator? He certainly believes in law and order--provided this doesn't apply to him or his cronies. He is a consummate hypocrite--not that this bothers him or his loyalists.

He joins a host of party faithful who believe having to testify under oath is alien to their being. To allude to a former president, if you have nothing to hide, why do you refuse to testify under oath? He won't answer that question; he's too busy taking to task the messenger, believing that deflecting to the messenger takes away the sting of the message.

Fortunately, he doesn't fool everybody. Ignoring subpoenas and the risk of having to testify truthfully under oath seems to be standard operating procedure among certain Republicans. Perhaps now we'll find out just how shady this poor excuse for a United States senator is, and how much above the law he is not.

WHAT HAPPENS WHEN GOVERNMENT FAILS

The words of our Declaration of Independence echo throughout our history: "We hold these truths to be self-evident, that all men are created equal, that they are endowed by their Creator with certain unalienable Rights, that among these are Life, Liberty and the pursuit of Happiness."

The First Amendment to our nation's Constitution protects five freedoms: speech, religion, press, assembly, and the right to petition the government.

These are bedrock, foundational principles deeply ingrained in our nation's conscience.

People generally turn to their government when they believe it's in their best interests. When the nation's economy tanked in the late 1920s, they turned to government for relief. When we faced world war, we turned to government to mobilize and fight to a successful outcome. There is no doubt of the bedrock historical relationship between our government and the governed. It has sustained us through tragedy and triumph for almost 250 years.

The people expect their city, county, state and federal representatives to look after their concerns and address them in a competent, efficient manner. They expect laws to be passed, and law enforcement to do their job, to keep us safe, so that we may all enjoy life, liberty and the pursuit of happiness through the rights granted in our Constitution, as well as other "inalienable rights" not specifically mentioned in our charter documents.

The most important duty of government is to keep its citizens safe through a system of law and order that is fair, understood, applied equally and followed.

But what happens when those glowing words noted above don't necessarily square with current life conditions?

We are a nation that exists based on the consent of the governed.

What happens:

When all men who are created equal nevertheless face different treatment under the law?

When life and liberty can be unlawfully taken, yet the perpetrators are set free?

When, in the name of freedom, government seeks to control what we think, say and do?

When freedom of speech is curtailed or prevented to avoid offending?

When religion means a particular religion?

When the number of newspapers continues to decline, and the press is assaulted as "the enemy of the people," while unaccountable and too often irresponsible social media gain traction as sources of fact?

When freedom of assembly is treated as violence and prevented?

When petitioning the government is met with silence?

When public safety is threatened at any time by acts of violence?

When police response to mass shootings is ineffective, or worse? (In Uvalde, police stood by for over an hour while the shooter holed up inside. In Illinois, the police had ample evidence of the instability and threats of violence by the perpetrator, yet did nothing because he wasn't reported by family members. Is this what we can expect from law enforcement before and after mass shootings occur?)

When Social Security is targeted by certain elements who proclaim they want to protect this lifeline program?

When the will of the voters can be trashed under an "Independent State Legislature Claim" that the Supreme Court will consider next term? Those who press this claim argue that since the Constitution doesn't name other parts of state government -- including courts -- they should have no power to check the legislature on the subject of federal elections. Even if a state's constitution or laws give power to courts or a governor, the theory argues legislatures should be able to ignore them. Imagine that, the state legislature setting aside the will of the voters in favor of its own political judgment!

If the legislative and executive branches of government are not responsive to public grievances, people look to the judiciary. But what happens when the judiciary is unresponsive?

A significant majority of Americans favor gun restrictions, including a ban on assault rifles. A significant majority also favors a woman's right to have an abortion under certain conditions. Yet, on these major issues, government is largely unresponsive. There are others where there is a divide between majority wants and minority grants.

In the eyes of many, it's a matter of favoring a minority religious and cultural view at the expense of a significant majority.

What holds our nation together is a rich tapestry of red, white and blue. But historians and pundits are telling us that, with each passing day, we are becoming red and blue, with each color deepening, with no overlap and a clear line of demarcation. In their words, we are becoming two nations with differing philosophies of governing, culture, and general way of life--and with each one pointing in defense of their views to the same Constitution.

What happens when the governed begin to question their consent?

As Abraham Lincoln said, "A nation divided against itself cannot stand." History tells us what happens when government is no longer responsive to the governed. Imagine if you will a large rug. Take a tool to that rug and begin ripping up the strands that bind it. In short order, what will that rug look like? Now, apply that to our national tapestry.

You get the picture.

SOME COMPARISONS BETWEEN CONSERVATIVES AND LIBERALS

In the 1920s, conservative economic policies led to the stock market crash of 1929, and the Great Depression.

Liberals enacted programs in the 1930s, such as Social Security, designed to get our economy back on track.

In the 1930s, conservatives favored appeasing Adolf Hitler, refusing critical aid to Great Britain.

Liberals aided Great Britain in its "darkest hour" and with the allies, defeated Hitler, Nazism and Fascism in World War II.

Since 2017, conservatives have endorsed white nationalist, neo-Nazi groups.

Liberals oppose these groups, saying there is no place in America for Nazism, Fascism or any other form of repressive, authoritarian government.

In 2021, conservatives led an attack on the nation's capital, seeking to overthrow the government and keep Donald Trump in power unconstitutionally and illegally, based on a lie now known as the Big Lie.

Liberals (and some moderate conservatives) are trying to hold these self-professed conservative "law and order" champions accountable and responsible for their criminal conduct.

Conservatives are dishonoring subpoenas, pleading the Fifth Amendment, and obstructing justice, claiming what happened on January 6 was nothing more than "legitimate public discourse."

Liberals (and some moderate conservatives) are trying to get these conservatives to adhere to the rule of law and be true to their claim of favoring individual accountability and responsibility.

Conservatives have re-written election laws designed to suppress targeted voting groups, and are seeking the Supreme Court's blessing on a theory that would allow state legislatures to override the will of the voting public in federal elections.

Liberals (and some moderate conservatives) believe the right to vote is a fundamental constitutional right set out in several amendments, and that conservatives are undermining this fundamental right, which would be irrevocably undermined if conservative state legislatures are given the power to reject the will of the state voters… which is precisely what Donald Trump, and his loyalists, wanted some states to do in 2020.

Conservatives are re-writing history. declaring in law what can and can't be taught; declaring in law what can and can't be said in the classroom and on college and university campuses.

Liberals are resisting conservative efforts at undermining our nation's historic commitment to teaching history's important lessons, warts and all; they vigorously support academic freedom and are resisting conservative efforts to undermine classroom instruction.

Conservatives favor banning books.

Liberals oppose any and all efforts at thought control by book banning.

Conservatives favor the church directing the state, or a theocracy.

Liberals favor a wall of separation between church and state that has sustained our nation since its founding.

Conservatives seek to undermine constitutional privacy rights.

Liberals believe in the protection of individual privacy rights as fundamental in an ordered society.

Conservatives favor making access to firearms more convenient, including concealed and open carry in places where the public congregates--even as the number of mass shootings is rising, and with more and more being killed and injured by gunfire.

Liberals favor common sense gun regulations, such as banning weapons of war on the streets, and more restrictive registration requirements to avoid loopholes.

WHAT MAKES MR. ALTERNATIVE A BETTER CHOICE?

I know several colleagues who are ardent Biden Bashers. They post comments, undoubtedly taken from various websites, that serve as Biden zings. Such things as he's demented, or he has amnesia or he's whatever the poke of the day says he is.

I am a firm believer in fair comment and criticism—indeed, this ability to write and speak lies at the very heart of the First Amendment. The ability to offer fair comment and criticism is one of the great freedoms that separates us from totalitarian regimes. And if people get their jollies by short zings in lieu of analytical comment and fact-based criticism, then why not? After all, who really cares?

In short, if it makes the bashers feel good, that's really all that matters to them.

But I want to challenge the Biden Bashers to do more than find little quips that make them feel good. I want them to tell me what it is that makes Mr. Alternative better.

Do the bashers believe him when he says he lost the election in 2020 because it was rigged?

Do the bashers agree when Mr. Alternative says there are some good Neo-Nazis?

Do the bashers support the Oath Keepers, Proud Boys and other white nationalist groups, as Mr. Alternative does?

Do the bashers favor eliminating the separation of church and state, thereby authorizing the church to direct the government?

Do the bashers favor government policies premised on Evangelical Christian religion?

Do the bashers support banning women from making decisions about their own well-being?

Do the bashers believe state legislators should determine the outcome of presidential elections regardless of the state vote totals?

Do the bashers support banning books and, if so, who should be responsible for book banning?

Do the bashers believe American history and civics should be re-written to remove parts that might be offensive? If so, who should be charged with this re-write?

Do the bashers believe any law-abiding citizen should be free to own an assault rifle and carry it on the public streets and roads?

Do the bashers believe Mr. Alternative didn't commit any offense related to his actions before, during and immediately after the January 6 assault on the capital?

I know answering these eleven questions requires some careful thought, but since those who support Mr. Alternative are such great, logical thinkers, this shouldn't present a difficult task for them at all. Answering these questions ought to be a piece of cake for them.

After all, any ignoramus can find little quips or puns or other quickie-type zings in a matter of minutes. They can do better than that by answering these few questions about Mr. Alternative—and in answering them, they will be saying much about themselves.

THE LEGAL NOOSE TIGHTENS

After seven televised public hearings by the House Select Committee investigating the January 6 attack on the nation's capital, certain things are now abundantly clear.

Claims by Donald Trump and his acolytes of a "witch hunt," or "hatchet job" ring hollow.

Most of Trump's staunch loyalists have become silent, their bombast largely missing in action.

The case against Trump has been made predominantly by conservative Republicans and Trump supporters who were led astray by a consummate con artist and pathological liar.

Those who chose to incur the wrath of the dwindling number of Trumpites are the true heroes who exhibited courage and strength to tell the truth under oath.

Those who continue to resist testifying under oath and otherwise snub their noses at accountability for their actions are the cowards and weaklings fearful of Trump and his steadfast crew. But Trump is losing his grip on some of those, and more and more of them will come forth and do what they should have been doing all along to save their own necks; testify under oath about Donald Trump.

It was almost 50 years ago when presidential advisor John Dean told President Richard Nixon that Watergate was a cancer on the presidency. Recall his exact words:

"We have a cancer--within, close to the Presidency, that's growing. It's growing daily. It's compounding, it grows geometrically now because it compounds itself." Watergate was a metastasizing scandal, but as bad as it was; as crooked as Richard Nixon was revealed to be, it pales in comparison to the disgrace and disgust Donald Trump brought to the presidency.

He is the most corrupt, dishonest, crooked president in American history. No other president has ever attacked the centerpiece of our nation's form of government. No other president has ever refused to acknowledge electoral defeat by knowingly creating a lie out of whole cloth, and encouraging violence for the sole purpose of staying power.

Donald Trump is a cancer on the nation's body politic. He was a cancer on the presidency.

Those who attacked the capital have faced, and are facing, their day of judgment. Many are behind bars.

Donald Trump belongs in jail. Those who aided and abetted his criminal enterprise belong in jail.

To be sure, they will be charged and prosecuted in due course. Americans still believe in responsibility and accountability, and Trump and his Trumpites who committed criminal acts will come face to face with our nation's legal system.

History will record with favor those who stood up to the MAGA madness and forged ahead with a diligent search for the truth about January 6.

Trump and Trumpism will face the wrath of history; he will be relegated to history's dustbin.

Trump will become Exhibit A for crookedness, sociopath personality traits, megalomania, and other behavioral weaknesses the profile of which should have never been near the presidency, much less elected to lead our nation.

He is a grossly flawed human being whose failings are many, and will only become more magnified over the next several weeks and months as the House committee peels away the layers to expose the corrupt core that lies within.

What is without question today is that he violated his oath of office and betrayed the principles on which our nation was founded.

As more and more decide to part ways with him and his ilk, it is hoped the Republican Party leaders will return to the true, guiding principles of conservatism in the mold of Barry Goldwater, William F. Buckley, Jr., and Ronald Reagan.

Trump is not, and never was, a conservative Republican in its true historical iteration. He is an authoritarian neo-Fascist who has, over the past several years, brought out the worst of us. He created a cult of Trumpites by stoking anger and resentment against those who "are different."

A president's role is to heal and bring together; Trump is anathema to that. His rhetoric is that of division, anger, hatred and conflict.

His biggest crime is putting himself above country. He will gladly sacrifice family, friend, colleague, etc., for his own self-promotion.

Our better angels have taken charge. Whether it's Georgia, New York, or the federal judicial system—or all of the above--Trump can no longer hide from the fate that awaits him. The wheels of justice grind exceedingly slow and exceedingly fine, but they do grind on.

The legal noose tightens. His time to pay the piper draws nigh.

"LOCK THEM UP": STRICT LIABILITY FOR PARENTS, ETC., AND GUN MANUFACTURERS AND SELLERS

In a "it's better than nothing" moment, Congress passed, and the president signed, the first major firearms legislation in more than a generation. This action was taken on the heels of two mass shootings in Texas and Illinois.

This supposed "feel good" legislation would most likely not have prevented these two mass murders, simply because it doesn't address the heart of the problem: easy access to weapons of mass murder.

The legislation expands background checks for 18–21-year-old prospective buyers. But what about parents, etc., who buy these weapons and leave them where their teenager can get his hands on them? Nothing there.

The legislation addresses domestic abuse. How many mass shootings involved domestic disputes? None that I can recall. The law allows for people who are restricted from gun access to have their rights to own a gun restored if they have a clean record for five years. How many mass shooters fit this profile? Again, I can't recall a single one.

The new law pushes states to enact red flag laws, allowing law enforcement to ask a court to take away guns from those deemed threats. Sadly, we saw how well this worked in the latest mass shooting in Illinois where one red flag after another was ignored. We've seen a lot of finger-pointing deflecting blame since then, but there is no accountability, and many innocent lives were lost. And the law doesn't mandate a state to adopt these laws anyway.

The new law also includes penalties for those who conduct straw purchases, the process of illegally buying a gun from another person. How many mass shootings have resulted from this type of purchase? I can't think of a single one.

And finally, there's the usual money for training and mental health. We saw how effective training was in the Uvalde, Texas shooting where finger-pointing by law enforcement has replaced accountability.

The sad fact is that, following these shootings, dots that could have easily been connected were ignored, or it was believed others were responsible for doing the connecting. There's a lot of second-guessing after these shootings, but it's far too little and far too late.

This new federal law will, to a large extent, have no bearing on situations where parents buy a weapon legally, leave it out for a teenage son to gain access, who then invades a place where people congregate.

Until there is a total ban on the sale of assault rifles to members of the public, and a universal background check on all sales of firearms, Congress and state legislatures will continue to dance around the subject of the epidemic of mass shootings.

What is needed are laws that impose strict liability on those involved in the process of these weapons of mass murder finding their way into the hands of a killer.

Strict liability should be a strong selling point for Republicans who have historically opposed more meaningful, common sense, gun regulation. Such a strict liability law would make people accountable for their actions, and we know a major

Republican talking point is holding people accountable and responsible for their actions.

Strict liability is nothing new; it's a legal doctrine that has been around for a very long time. Strict liability exists when a defendant is liable for committing an action, regardless of what his/her intent or mental state was when committing the action. In criminal law, possession crimes and statutory rape are both examples of strict liability offenses.

Other offenses include selling alcohol to minors and traffic offenses. A person who sells alcohol to a minor can be convicted even if the seller had a belief that the person was old enough to buy alcohol.

The theory behind strict liability is that it does not depend on actual negligence but is based on the breach of an absolute duty to make something safe. What can be government's greatest duty than protecting people from mass gun violence?

California Governor Gavin Newsom recently signed legislation allowing the state, local governments and Californians to sue gun makers. A strict liability law could add parents, guardians or caregivers who legally purchase a firearm, but fail to safely secure it, thereby allowing for easy access.

"To the victims of gun violence and their families: California stands with you. The gun industry can no longer hide from the devastating harm their products cause," Governor

Newsom said. "Our kids, families and communities deserve streets free of gun violence and gun makers must be held accountable for their role in this crisis. Nearly every industry is held liable when people are hurt or killed by their products – guns should be no different."

"Gun violence is now the leading cause of death among kids and teens in the United States, surpassing car accidents. I see no better argument for stronger gun safety legislation. For far too long, the firearms industry has enjoyed federal immunity from civil lawsuits, providing them no incentive for them to follow our laws. Hitting their bottom line may finally compel them to step up to reduce gun violence by preventing illegal sales and theft."

California Attorney General Rob Bonta said: "There have been more mass shootings in our nation than days in the year, and yet many members of the gun industry continue to use a combination of bullying, exploitation, and fear to rack up profits from the very tools used in these shootings. There is no reason that the gun industry should be the only industry exempt from responsibility for the harm that its products cause, especially when its products are responsible for the deaths of thousands of Americans each year.

Imposing fines on gun manufacturers will have some effect, but they can pass along these fines to the consumers.

What really needs to be done is to refer to that famous refrain from several years ago: lock them up. Pass criminal laws that hold those involved strictly liable. And don't give parents, etc., a slap on the wrist; lock them up. Hold them accountable.

Imprisonment will get their attention. Guaranteed.

ARE THERE CONSERVATIVES WHO CAN RELEGATE THE EXTREME ELEMENTS TO HISTORY'S DUSTBIN?

In a "what took them so long?" moment, several more moderate conservative thinkers reached a conclusion that was obvious to tens of millions of us more than a year and a half ago: Biden won, Trump lost. While the Big Lie sadly angered millions that led to violence at our nation's capital, it is hoped that more traditional dispassionate conservative thinkers will replace the overt bigotry and hatred that has metastasized into the extreme right wing of the Republican Party.

There is no doubt that the history of the current version of Republican extremism is steeped in religious fervor, and is anti-Black, anti-Semitism, anti-immigration—in sum, right wing extremists oppose everything that they believe is a threat to "them." Beginning with the right-wing assault on the New Deal, conservatives have used the mantra of "State's rights" as a subterfuge or dog whistle for rank bigotry, hatred and violence. The KKK, McCarthyism and the fake communist witch hunt, right wing opposition to civil rights and voting rights legislation, white nationalist groups spreading their bigotry and bile, and on and on. The sad, tragic history is there in the books to read and learn. Is there any secret to the right wing's fervor in wanting to re-write or abolish its harsh teachings completely? They will learn, however, that history can't be hidden; it can't be sanitized. Truth has a way of rearing its head, as ugly as that is to the extremists who now control the Republican Party.

MORE SECRECY FROM THE DISGRACED TRUMP ADMINISRATION

Secret Service deleted texts during a two-day period that covered the January 6 attack on the nation's capital. Here is another example of the lack of transparency, openness and honesty of the Trump Administration. Fortunately, it shouldn't be that difficult to get to the bottom of this. Simply find out who was on duty, who made the decisions, and issue subpoenas for them to testify under oath. If they evade or obstruct, initiate the process of removing these people from government employment, and investigate them for possible criminal prosecution. 18 U.S.C. Secs. 641, 1519 and 2071 deal with destruction of public records.

A FETUS AS A PERSON: "UNINTENDED CONSEQUENCES?"

A Texas woman claims her unborn baby should count as a passenger in high occupant vehicle lane on the highway. This is an interesting take on personhood. If a fetus is considered a person at the time of conception, then what rights or benefits does this person have at that time? The abortion decision may turn out to be an example of the law of unintended consequences. Or perhaps in the "be careful what you wish for" category.

AN INCREDIBLE STORY; AN UNFORGETTABLE WEEKEND---COURTESY OF DNA

Last weekend, my wife Harriet and I, along with our daughter Lani, my son-in-law Brian and their daughter Kelsie, visited my niece, nephew-in-law, three grandnieces and their family in Connecticut for an unforgettable weekend. What made this visit unforgettable is that, until June of last year, I didn't know I had a niece, nephew-in-law and grandnieces!

Now here is the story. My brother Barry married his childhood sweetheart Anne in 1969; he passed away from cancer in 1984 at age 36. The story that I carried with me for more than 50 years was that he had cancer for the last 15 years of his life, and that the treatment for his cancer prevented him from fathering a child.

It turns out the story is true; but the timeline was off.

Barry married his high school sweetheart Anne in June of 1969. It was a quickly cobbled together wedding in Miami Beach. I flew down from Tallahassee to be his best man. There were only about 16 people who attended. After the wedding, Barry and his wife left for Tampa, where he was attending college. He was subsequently drafted, but received a medical discharge because he contracted Hodgkin's Disease sometime around 1971 or 1972.

He eventually gained his Ph.D. in Audiology from the University of Maryland and became an audiologist with the Veterans Administration, first in Washington, D.C. and then in Miami.

Flash forward to June of last year. Harriet and I went to North Carolina for my granddaughter Kelsie's high school graduation. While Harriet and Kelsie's sister Hailey went shopping and everyone else was out of the house, My daughter Lani, who is big into Ancestry and DNA, took me into her office at home and asked me if I knew a Sara Kish. I told her I'd never heard that name before.

Then, she slowly unraveled the most incredible story of my life. She told me she was contacted by Sara, who emailed Lani and told her that Sara's DNA test showed her to be a close match with my daughter—first cousin close!

Lani first explained to me how Sara could only have been born of a sibling of mine and a sibling of his wife Anne. I had only one sibling--Barry. So did

Anne. The realization hit me like a ton of bricks.

Then she showed me the adoption agency report that described Sara's birth parents. That report described my brother and Anne to a T. She then showed me a picture of Sara, who is the image of her birth mother! I then saw a picture of Sara's family; their youngest daughter Ashlyn definitely has Barry's features.

With each revelation, my jaw dropped further and further. Lani then asked what I was going to do. "Why call her," was my immediate answer.

When I did, I was greeted with "Hello Uncle George" from Sara and her three girls, Alexa, Ava and Ashlyn. Yes, the tears flowed. I was an uncle and granduncle! Never in my life could I have imagined such a thing!

At the time Barry and Anne married, she was already past six months pregnant. Sara was born in Tampa in late August of 1969 and immediately adopted and moved out of Florida.

I came to find out that Sara had been searching for her birth parents for many years. Her late adoptive father, and her adoptive mother, encouraged her search. Unfortunately, it wasn't until much later than DNA searches had become perfected.

When Sara found a match with Anne's sister, she emailed Lani, who quickly connected the dots.

Since June of 2021, I have been in constant contact with Sara, her husband Michael, and their girls. I am officially Uncle G. I signed my email that way once, and it's clicked.

We found incredible similarities. They love hockey and are big New York Rangers fans. So am I; my dad used to take Barry and me to Rangers games in the 1950s.

Harriet's birthday is July 9; Alexa's birthday is the same day.

Lani has two daughters, Hailey 21 and Kelsie 19. My other daughter Amy and son-in-law Frank have two children, Avery 13 and Connor 10 in August.

Sara's daughters are 21, 17 and 12.

Sara's adoptive father passed away from leukemia; Barry's cause of death was leukemia.

I knew that eventually, we would all meet. Sara has a busy life, with Michael and three active, involved girls. But finally, we found the weekend of July 8 convenient for them and Lani. (Since Harriet and I are retired, convenience isn't a problem for us.)

So, we flew to Hartford and drove to the south. We initially met at the hotel where we stayed, and the first meeting began a three-day lovefest. It was as if we knew each other as family for many years.

We spent the weekend partying and sharing stories. Harriet and I met Sara's adoptive mother, Michael's parents, and other family members and friends. I lost count of the hugs and kisses.

I still get goosebumps whenever I think of this magic weekend. To know that my beloved brother lives on through his daughter and granddaughters is overwhelming. Our cherished father never knew he had a third granddaughter, and now has seven great-grandchildren.

I consider myself blessed to know this, particularly since I am well into my senior years.

I will treasure last weekend for the rest of my life. I am indeed an incredibly lucky guy to have a niece, nephew-in-law and three grandnieces, and their families.

We are family!

DESPICABLE THEM

Never mind dealing with the significant problems besetting our nation. Never mind being faithful to their oaths of office as elected public servants. These rabid right-wing extremists have one mission in mind should they gain control of the House of Representatives in this year's elections: revenge for their lord and master, Donald Trump.

Never mind the overwhelming evidence of criminal conduct presented by Republican witnesses before the House select committee investigating the January 6 attack on the capital. Never mind the role of Congress to investigate for the purpose of uncovering what happened, and enact laws to prevent a reoccurrence.

What matters to the Kevin McCarthys and Jim Jordans is pure and simple revenge against those who showed the courage and fortitude to testify publicly under oath and tell the truth.

Of course, McCarthy, Jordan and their kind have yet to show similar courage. And they won't as long as they have enough supporters who believe every word they say and are convinced that what they see and hear--assuming some are watching the hearings--is not reality; rather, what Trump, McCarthy and Jordan say is their reality.

These disgraceful members of Congress are nothing more than Trump lackeys who are cowards when it comes to telling the truth and owning up to the criminality of their own conduct.

Here is a classic example of their cowardice and inanity. There was a report about a 10-year-old rape victim who had to leave her home state of Ohio to get an abortion in Indiana. Typically, the rabid right wing exploded, with one of its chief cheerleaders, Jordan, claiming it was a lie and actually blamed Joe Biden for this. Not to be outdone, the Ohio attorney general chimed in, saying it was a lie. Their responses were no doubt targeted to arouse the anger and resentment of their base; they are good at whipping up a frenzy to mouth-foaming fervor. Indeed, considering their lack of policy initiatives designed to address the concerns of the significant majority, whipping up their masses is what they do best.

Well, facts do have a way of interfering with their lunacy, and eventually, the story was proven to be true. What did Jordan say about this when confronted with the truth? He simply said he never said what he is quoted as saying. Real leadership here. Real courage.

A real phony.

These characters would make great circus clowns if their actions didn't seriously undermine our system of government. They have taken it upon themselves to decide for us what our democracy is to be. They have taken it upon themselves to decide what liberty, freedom and justice mean for the rest of us.

They favor a nation of men, not of laws.

They need to be called out for what they really are; an existential threat to our form of government that has so far survived almost 250 years.

They are despicable characters, and the rest of us can only hope that our system of justice prevails. If our system holds, many of the plotters and revenge-seekers will be under indictment facing trial for their crimes against our nation.

For the time being, we must leave it to our better angels--those who have testified before the select committee; those yet to testify; those charged with upholding the laws of our nation and several states; and those who find the behavior of Trump and his congressional comrades and other sycophants to be despicable.

Our nation depends on our system of justice to function as it has since our Founding Fathers established it in our Constitution. To be sure, it has faced stressful moments in our history; but it has held fast.

It is being tested now by these low-lives; but sooner or later those who break the law or snub their noses at it must face the music. And the orchestra is playing.

DEFLECTION, DEFLECTION, DEFLECTION

In 2016, Donald Trump was handed the keys to the White House when a report was issued that revealed that during Hillary Clinton's years as secretary of state (2009-2013), she used her private email account to conduct government business.

On the heels of the attack at Benghazi, Trump seized the initiative. You might remember the familiar chant during campaign stops: "Lock her up." Trump whipped his crowds into a frenzy with this chant. It was great theater. And it worked. In tandem with his pitch to the effect that no one avoids testifying under oath or pleads the Fifth Amendment if they have nothing to hide, Trump made his way to the White House.

From 2017 to 2021, Donald Trump and the Republican Party controlled the Department of Justice and the 93 united states attorneys' offices throughout the country, the chief criminal prosecutorial arm of the federal government.

How many indictments did they file against Hillary Clinton? How many charges did they bring against her, either resulting from the attack at Benghazi or from the use of her private email account to conduct government business?

ZERO!!

Not to be outdone, during the leadup to the 2020 presidential election, Trump and his cronies focused on Hunter Biden's, Joe Biden's son, in connection with the former's dealings in Ukraine. You remember Trump's telephone call to the Ukraine president asking for dirt on Biden in return for the release of congressionally authorized funds to help shore up the Ukraine military. This self-professed "perfect" call by Trump led to his first impeachment.

For the better part of Trump's last two years in office, he and his party controlled the Justice Department and the entire federal prosecutorial system. How many indictments were issued against Hunter Biden? How many charges were filed against him?

ZERO!!

While still in office, Trump appointed a Republican federal prosecutor, John Durham, to investigate Hunter Biden. When Joe Biden was elected, rather than firing Durham, which was in his rights to do so, Biden retained Durham to complete his investigation.

In the more than two years that Durham has been investigating, the only charge he filed was against a Democrat lawyer, Michael Sussman, who was charged with one count of lying to the FBI. Sussman went on trial and was acquitted of this single charge.

Now comes China. Trump has conflated his accusations against former Vice President Joe Biden and son Hunter Biden -- railing against Hunter Biden's business dealings, then saying that Joe Biden "takes a billion-five" from China and "he goes on and he allows China to rip us off." He added, "So the Bidens got rich while America got robbed." Trump does have a way of, shall we say, exaggerating or inflating his claims. He's a master at that.

Unfortunately for Trump, there is no evidence Joe Biden has received large sums of money from China or has otherwise gained wealth as a result of his son's business dealings abroad.

Trump has previously made the "billion-five" accusation against Hunter Biden. While a conservative author has used this figure, it has not been proven. A lawyer for Hunter Biden, George Mesires, says the investment company in which Hunter Biden has an equity stake was capitalized with a total of about $4.2 million at today's exchange rates, "not $1.5 billion." Even this investment was not a direct payment to Hunter Biden; Hunter Biden holds a 10% stake in the firm, Mesires says, and has not made a profit to date.

So, with Republicans in charge of the prosecutorial machinery, what have they gotten on Clinton and the Bidens? Nothing. And they spent millions to get that zero result.

But since Trump is facing far more serious charges arising out of his conduct as president, and his loyalists in and out of Congress are also in the criminal justice spotlight, deflection from their plight is their calling card.

While their feckless efforts to equate Biden with Trump are failing—Biden never led an insurrection against our government; he never tried to overthrow our government---even Republicans realize that to make a case in court, you need facts and law. And neither Trump nor his loyalists had either facts or law in Clinton's case, and so far, the same is true regarding Hunter Biden. The lack of facts and law in the more than 60 cases they lost trying to overturn the presidential election says volumes about the Republican Party's quality of legal expertise and its willingness to make fools of themselves.

Of course, this won't stop the rabid Republicans from going after them—especially Biden—should they reclaim the House of Representatives. The party's leadership has made that abundantly clear. Moreover, they will go after those members of the select committee investigating the January 6 attack on the capital for daring to question the actions of their party's wayward leader and his band of insurrectionists.

Our nation has serious problems that must be addressed by our government leaders; sadly, we know what the Republican agenda calls for—revenge. And the Republicans have the temerity to call this leadership!

They will continue to deflect, seeking out strawmen or conjuring up bogeymen wherever the can. Recall the final scenes of that great movie "The Wizard of Oz." The current version of the Republican Party will do everything it can to keep the public's eye off the man behind the curtain pulling the strings.

But truth has a way of rearing its head. Trump and his cronies can avoid testifying under oath. They can plead the Fifth Amendment. We all know they're hiding something. Trump said that when it was Hillary Clinton in the spotlight. Now, it's him and his ilk that are facing their day of reckoning. What goes around, comes around.

Who are they fooling? Not the vast majority of Americans. The MAGA crowd of loyalists…whose numbers have been dropping as revelations mount.

So, deflect away! Promise more deflections. Your loyalists will buy anything you sell. But make no mistake about it, your number is coming up.

WHAT ABOUT JOE BIDEN? DON'T UNDERESTIMATE HIM.

More than a year and a half into his first term, there is much speculation about Joe Biden's future. He will be 80 years old later this year; he is not aging well. Known for gaffes even as a 36-year member of the U.S. Senate, they are magnified now in his advancing years.

He faces criticism from Republicans and Democrats alike. Republicans gleefully declare him "senile" or "suffering from dementia." Democrats are more circumspect, saying he's not demonstrating the stamina necessary to do the job.

His party faces the prospect of significant losses in the House of Representatives, and he may lose the barest of majorities in the Senate. (Indeed, with two senators, Joe Manchin and Krysten Sinema, more helpful to the Republican Party than to the Democrats, even a return of the current senate balance will be of no help to Biden.)

His Build Back Better plan faces the scrapheap after the November election cycle. The Republican-led House has promised to conduct investigations seeking revenge against Democrats generally, including efforts to impeach Biden regardless of its factual and legal justification. (Remember, this is the Republican Party of alternative facts, and its lack of legal acumen was clearly demonstrated during the post-presidential election period when Trump and his allies lost every lawsuit they filed seeking to overturn the election.

It was only after they lost in court that they resorted to violence.)

In short, nothing will stop Republican efforts to exact their revenge against those who had and have the audacity to call out Trump and the virulence of Trumpism.

In the mid-to-late 1960s, anger-fueled protests raged across America over the Vietnam war. Yet, it wasn't until March of 1968—just a few months before the election--that President Lyndon Johnson declared he wouldn't seek reelection. In short, he decided not to become a lame duck until he realized he could wait no longer if his party was to have any chance of winning the White House.

Joe Biden does not want to be a two-year lame duck president. Under normal circumstances, no president would end his own political relevancy by such a self-inflicted wound.

But these are not normal times.

Biden and the Democrats face rampant inflation; they appear unable to craft a message that clearly identifies what the party stands for; and they haven't done anything to arouse and energize their base.

The House select committee investigation into January 6 has opened some eyes, exposing how they were played by Trump and his great con game, but how that is reflected in actual votes remains to be seen. We also know what to expect should the Republicans reclaim at least one house of Congress, but it's a risky choice for the Democrats to put all their eggs into that one basket. Pointing out criminal conduct, expressing outrage over criminal behavior, and turning evidence over for criminal prosecution are proper actions, but whether this translates to enough votes is a different matter altogether. After all, history shows that people generally vote their pocketbook. Recall Bill Clinton's successful "It's the economy, stupid" line from his campaign chief.

But Biden has one great advantage his critics don't have: he is the president of the United States.

Even under a worst-case scenario, he still has one thing that gives him a huge advantage: the veto pen. While he won't be able to pass anything during the next two years if things go south for him in November, neither will the Republicans, even if they capture both houses of Congress. They simply won't have enough votes to override a presidential veto. This may force the Republicans to negotiate with him. Imagine that; Republicans forced to negotiate with the Democrats to get anything passed!

What could conceivably force Biden's hand and make him a long-term lame duck is whether, after November, enough members of his own party in Congress convince him to announce early on that he won't be a candidate in 2024. This would certainly give party hopefuls ample time to make their case for the nomination.

But Biden may want to see what becomes of Trump and his allies following the hearings. He may want to see how the criminal justice system handles the congressional revelations. He may also want to see what the potential party field looks like in terms of his successor. Both of these may not materialize until late 2023 or even early 2024. Or he may turn stubborn and just want to hold out until the last possible moment, like LBJ did. Time is on his side, whether Republicans and potential Democrat candidates like it or not.

The bottom line is that Biden has nothing to lose. Even an impeachment will look like what it is—Democrats will call it a vindictive baseless hatchet job that just might anger the party's base going into 2024; Republicans will say it is deserved after what the Democrats did to Trump. In other words, the ball is not going to move on this, unless there is a revolt over a misuse of the process, whereby every future president faced with the opposition party in the House will in turn face impeachment whether justified or not. What this would do to undermine our democracy should be self-evident, but with revenge the goal, this might not matter.

Whatever decision he makes, the ball is still in Biden's court. Until January 20, 2025, he is in charge of the executive branch of government, including the Justice Department and the federal prosecutorial offices.

To those who count him out as irrelevant, remember this: no one in the history of our nation served longer in public office before being elected president. No one serves six terms in the senate and two terms as vice president without having the savvy and skills to navigate the twists and turns of our political system, even to the point of pulling political rabbits out of the hat.

Those who count him out do so their peril.

Every one of Biden's cabinet officers are responsible to him. He appointed them, and they are required to be answerable to him. This is especially true of key departments such as state, defense, homeland security, and justice. To believe that Biden isn't aware of the relationship between the January 6 committee and the justice department is to believe in the truth of wild conspiracy theories. (Well, maybe this isn't the best analogy.) Think about those briefing sessions he has with his cabinet officers. More specifically, think about those briefing sessions between Biden White House staff and the Justice Department—including the FBI.

As president, he commands the vast expanse and enormous powers of the executive branch of the federal government.

After 36 years in the Senate, eight as vice president, assured of one full term as president, in his 80s and perhaps free from having to run again after reaching the height of his political career, he will be unshackled, liberated from the trappings of office.

At that point, he may simply decide to have some of his own payback during his last two years in public office. He will be free to use that veto pen, generally tick off Republicans by issuing executive orders and granting pardons, use the full expanse of the bully pulpit that is the office itself, and generally do whatever it takes to assure "that the laws be faithfully executed," including referrals to conduct investigations against those he believes are violating the law.

Until the moment he leaves office, he will retain the power to "faithfully execute the Office of President of the United States" and "preserve, protect and defend the Constitution of the United States." In short, until January 20, 2025, he will have the power to exact his own form of revenge, should he choose to do so.

Or he may just decide to run again!

WHERE IS THE SOCIALISM?

The most successful chant used by the Republicans against the Democrats is the cry of "socialism." Whenever the right wants to arouse its base, stoking them to anger, all the right has to do is utter the word "socialism" and promise that so long as the voters elect Republicans, there will never be socialism in America.

Since the administration of Woodrow Wilson, Democrats controlled the White House and Congress for a total of almost 44 years. Wilson (6), Franklin Roosevelt (12), Harry Truman (6), John Kennedy and Lyndon Johnson (8), Jimmy

Carter (4), Bill Clinton (2) and Barack Obama (2) and Joe Biden (going on 2).

Where is the socialism Republicans fear?

Some who have a measure of comprehension of American history will point out that Roosevelt's "New Deal" was all about socialism. Let's look at those pesky facts that are overlooked when Republicans use one word to whip up their base.

When the stock market crashed in 1929, tens of millions of Americans lost everything. Republicans had no plan to address the worst economic crisis in our history, except to maintain the status quo, meaning let the economy recover on its own. Leave business to its own devices; the law of supply and demand will assure recovery. From 1929 to early 1933, the Republicans were content to continue this laissez faire attitude toward business—the same attitude that led to the market collapse in the first place. Putting it bluntly, for the Republicans the cure was to continue the illness.

Roosevelt's "New Deal" was directed at the tanked economy. Major federal programs and agencies were created, including the Civilian Conservation Corps (CCC), the Civil Works Administration (CWA), the Farm Security Administration (FSA), the National Industrial Recovery Act of 1933 (NIRA) and the Social Security Administration (SSA). They provided support for farmers, the unemployed, youth, and the elderly. The New Deal included new constraints and safeguards on the banking industry and efforts to re-inflate the economy after prices had fallen sharply. New Deal programs included both laws passed by Congress as well as presidential executive orders during the first term of FDR's presidency.

The programs focused on what historians refer to as the "3 R's": relief for the unemployed and for the poor, recovery of the economy back to normal levels, and reform of the financial system to prevent a repeat depression. The New Deal produced a political realignment, making the Democratic Party the majority (as well as the party that held the White House for seven out of the nine presidential terms from 1933 to 1969) with its base in progressive ideas. The Republicans were split, with progressive Republicans in support but conservatives opposing the entire New Deal as hostile to business and economic growth.

To be sure, it took World War II's unprecedented mobilization to eventually move our country beyond and out of the economic woes of the "Great Crash." But even our efforts to take on Nazi Germany and Fascist Italy were met with strong resistance from the Republican conservatives, who favored appeasing Hitler. This opposition was driven to silence when Japan attacked Pearl Harbor on December 7, 1941. Declarations of war followed in rapid succession.

Back to my question. Where is this horrible, evil, wicked socialism that conservatives fear, and use as a weapon against the Democrats whenever they can?

After tackling that question, ask this one: what would the conservatives do? Eliminate social security? Unemployment compensation? Workers' compensation? How about LBJ's "Great Society" programs such as Medicare and Medicaid? Would the conservatives want to eliminate them? The Supplemental Social Security program introduced in 1973 greatly reduced poverty among the disabled. Would the conservatives want to eliminate this program?

We know what the Republicans think of Obamacare. They tried every which way to prevent its passing, and after it passed, spent millions of taxpayer's dollars to eliminate it through the courts. More than 14.5 million Americans signed up for Obamacare health insurance for 2022, a 21% jump over last year and the highest since the Affordable Care Act was signed 12 years ago.

Republicans have become largely silent about Obamacare. I suppose with the millions who have benefitted from it, Republicans are concerned about arousing the ire of millions of voters by taking away their medical benefits.

And while on the subject of health care, where is the Republican plan to replace Obamacare? Indeed, where is the Republican plan for health insurance generally? They have never offered one, and they never will. For conservatives, it's all about business. Tax benefits, other forms of special treatment for businesses—benefits for them not available for the rest of us. Corporate welfare is fine; financial assistance for the poor, and the struggling and declining middle class is forbidden. After all, that's really the socialism the Republicans are against, not the corporate kind.

But what about the other programs? Will conservatives go after them the way they went after abortion, and are now threatening to go after other Supreme Court decisions such as contraceptives, same sex marriages and other civil unions?

The next time the conservatives scream "socialism," ask two simple questions: what programs are providing you with benefits, and what programs do they want to eliminate? Since people generally vote their pocketbook, ask what financial benefits conservatives want to take out of your pocketbook. All in the name of socialism, of course.

WHAT ARE THE REPUBLICANS SELLING?

Polls show the voters aren't buying what the Democrats are selling. Inflation, gas prices and crime are the Republican selling points, along with their age-old rallying cry and major bugaboo, socialism. We can expect more of this type of emotion-driven by factually devoid campaigning as we move toward the November elections.

With rising prices and increasing crime rates, voters are naturally angry at the party in power. The anger over these two major issues is fueling a backlash against the party in power, which by default favors the party out of power.

Never mind that the power is largely illusory, considering the Senate Democrats-in-name-only Joe Manchin and Kyrsten Sinema have been blocking most of the Biden agenda.

But let's flip the question. What are the Republicans selling that many voters find so attractive? Perhaps the biggest selling point is that they're not Democrats. But what about policies that translate to programs? Political party leaders shouldn't run on what they oppose; rather, they should run and, if elected, deliver on what they promise in the form of legislation.

Let's start with inflation. Why are prices so high? Recall the old supply-and-demand cycle. When demand is high, prices go up. When demand is low, prices go down in the hopes of spurring greater demand. Should that increase in demand materialize, what happens to prices? Why they go up.

Why does this happen? The answer is an easy one. Businesses are ultimately geared toward one overarching end: profits. If businesses lose money, chances are they won't be in business very long. Breaking even may be ok, but over the long haul, breaking even isn't financially sustainable.

If the product or service that is offered is of sufficient quality, people will buy to the level they can afford, perhaps even going in debt to make the purchase. People are by nature consumers, and businesses depend on consumption.

The importance of purchasing power can't be overstated. Republicans, however, generally oppose a set minimum wage that produces a livable income. They believe that increasing the minimum wage works against businesses' bottom line. They believe that greater profits will result in greater investment. We all know the history of trickle-down economics: profits take precedence over investment.

And, with regard to a higher minimum wage, business opposition remains even though they are quite capable of passing along those increases to the consumer. But businesses have to be careful not to price themselves out of the market.

This is the great balancing act businesses must adhere to. A product's or service's price must be attractive enough to assure a positive bottom line, yet not be so high as to be largely unaffordable.

From this brief analysis, the question naturally arises: what will the Republicans do to reduce inflation? Since government can't force or control demand, and doesn't set prices, it can't raise or lower them. But through certain federal actions, like the Federal Reserve lowering or increasing interest rates, the government can influence prices, which in turn will influence demand.

Businesses favor the Republican Party. This should come as no surprise. Republicans provide for a better business climate by generally opposing those programs proffered by Democrats that provide benefits for the vast majority of Americans--including Republicans of course—such as health care, social programs, dealing with climate change and environmental issues, infrastructure repair and maintenance, etc. Republicans certainly don't want the voters to focus on the benefits they're receiving from Democrat-initiated programs, such as Social Security, Medicare, etc.

What businesses can do, however, is create an environment where demand is heightened, such as keeping products from reaching the market for eventual sale. Recall those container ships stalled in the waters off the coast. Was this a deliberate act? Recall gasoline products being withheld from the sellers. Was this a deliberate act, blamed perhaps conveniently on the Russian invasion of Ukraine? The point is speculation mounts when these situations occur.

When gas prices soared many years ago, this was blamed on a "gas shortage." When the crisis ended and gas prices stabilized, where did all of this "new" gas come from? Another planet?

The ultimate question on this point is whether there is some form of understanding between the Republican Party and Big Business that, in return for favorable action such as tax benefits, Big Business will create conditions that could spur inflation.

The point here is that ours is a managed economy, and businesses are quite capable of doing their part in the management process.

Next up is crime. What are the Republicans selling here? Rampant crime on the streets? States controlled by Republicans have higher murder rates than blue states, according to a new study by Third Way, a center-left public policy think tank based in Washington, D.C.

While Republicans have focused on big-city crime as a crucial midterm election platform, Third Way released a survey of state murder rates from 2020, the latest year available for such statistics.

The study says that the six states with the highest per-capita murder rates all voted for Donald Trump in 2020, as did eight of the top 10 states.

"Mississippi had the highest homicide rate at 20.50 murders per 100,000 residents, followed by Louisiana at 15.79, Kentucky at 14.32, Alabama at 14.2, and Missouri at 14. The national average was 6.5 per 100,000 residents, but the top five states had rates more than twice that high," the survey said.

I doubt you'll hear the Republicans trumpet this.

And then there are those mass shootings, those involving the use of a military style weapon Republicans refuse to ban from sale to the general public.

Is this an example of their crime-fighting agenda?

But what else will they sell on crime? Their efforts on this front are compromised by the criminal activities now under investigation by the House January 6 select committee. They can hardly point with pride to their party loyalists who are doing everything they can to avoid testifying under oath, relying on the Fifth Amendment right to remain silent, or those who sought a pardon from former president Trump. What examples of crime will they point to that doesn't reflect back on the questionable actions by some of the party faithful?

The conservatives will tell their party faithful that the Democrats are evil, radical, socialistic, etc. We know the game plan.

Please tell us what the conservative legislative proposals are. The Republicans must tell us what they will do to combat inflation, and reduce the crime rate.

Americans want action; they don't want anger as a substitute for action.

WHAT IS CAUSING INFLATION?

With inflation gripping our nation, we are angry and frustrated. We want to know why costs are so high. There are numerous articles that discuss the stark relationship between rising costs and corporate profits. Sadly, however, these articles don't get the kind of broad coverage needed to truly educate the public because they aren't glitzy or simple enough; discussions about economic require analysis and thought. There simply isn't enough red meat here to arouse universal resentment.

But the classic line is applicable here: follow the money. The unprecedented level of corporate profits while consumers suffer from rising costs is similar for oil companies; just check out the various sites for information on Big Oil profits as gas prices soar.

The bottom line is there are those making a financial killing out of inflation; we are entitled to know who they are, and what is being done about it; specifically, what is being done to rein in these huge profits at the expense of the consumers? Congress can act, but there are members of Congress who either support soaring corporate profits, or simply turn a blind eye to them. Most of us know who they are.

Sadly, they depend on a dumbed down electorate that either doesn't know or doesn't care who the culprits really are.

WHEN GOVERNMENT FAILS

The latest poll on government dissatisfaction reveals an ominous trend. The headline is most glaring: "Biden Approval Hits New Low Amid Public Discontent With Both Parties, Quinnipiac University National Poll Finds; Nearly Half Of Americans Worry About Being Mass Shooting Victim."

With regard to Congress and the Supreme Court, the poll notes "Americans send a message that echoes through the High Court and the Halls of Congress: You are not getting the job done. The Republicans hit a new high on disapproval, the Democrats fare little better, and SCOTUS is met with unprecedented disapproval."

On mass shootings, the poll finds "Imagine waking up every morning worried that you might be targeted in a mass killing. Nearly half of your fellow Americans say they live with that fear every day."

To say this is not a healthy sign in the relationship between the government and the governed would be a gross understatement. People are angry and restless.

Historically, we are a nation in which the government functions with the consent of the governed. But what happens when that consent is called into question by distrust and, even worse, anger and hatred?

When legislation is passed that benefit some, but alienate others? When executive actions favor some, while harming others? When court decisions support some, but enrage others? In the past, where there was disagreement with government action, we begrudgingly accepted the results. Witness Bush v. Gore. Does this same spirit exist today? It certainly doesn't look like it.

Added to this is yet another question: How is confidence in government to be maintained or restored when people live in fear of being victims of mass shootings and other crimes? How are people to react when they believe that government is failing in its most important job, keeping us safe?

When anger, rage and fear replace dialogue, facts, reason and common sense, how does government calm the waters and regain the public's confidence?

The great, if unspoken, consequence of rampant and roiling distrust is that it will force people to take matters into their own hands. If they can't trust government to either solve problems or let the people solve their problems under an agreed-upon system of law, then the "law of the street" or vigilantism rules the day.

The consequences of that should be starkly self-evident.

The causes of this distrust are in our nature; we are a nation that has long been considered a "melting pot," a blend of people from every corner of the world who fled oppression in their homeland and saw America as a promise of liberty and freedom—the American Dream. Recall the words on the Statue of Liberty: "Give me your tired, your poor, Your huddled masses yearning to breathe free, The wretched refuse of your teeming shore."

The words of the Declaration of Independence, the Preamble to our Constitution and the Pledge of Allegiance talk about inalienable rights; all are created equal; one nation under God; and liberty, freedom and justice for all.

But in giving life to those words, different groups give them different meanings. By way of example, it took several constitutional amendments to breathe life into those words, and even after the adoption of those amendments, our history tells of unequal application and treatment.

Different groups have different histories, different philosophies and different views of government's role and the relationship between government and its people. And those differences are more magnified now than they have ever been.

The causes of the discontent can be summed up in a simple phrase: "Different strokes for different folks." People are different, and some individuals or groups have different needs and wants from others. Giving to one is viewed as taking from another.

The reality check here is that we have always been different; yet, what has bound us as one nation historically was the commitment to the ideals that led to its formation. There have been times when, whatever differences existed, we came together when the national interest called for unity. World Wars I and II are the most obvious examples.

But the thread that weaves us together seems to be unraveling. North and South, left and right, have taken on tribal meanings.

It's as if the nation is searching for a single voice, a voice of reason to calm emotions and restore confidence in our form of government forged by our forefathers almost 250 years ago. But if history is a teacher, we know that where there is a leadership vacuum, what fills that vacuum is not a voice of reason; all too often, it is the voice of the authoritarian who promises great things, but delivers despotism.

We are facing choices. One thing is clear; our nation can't be sustained in an environment filled with anger, hatred, rancor and bitterness.

A POSSIBLE SOLUTION TO THE ABORTION DILEMMA?

There is no question that abortion is the hottest of hot-button social and moral issues engulfing our nation.

What compounds this issue is the apparent non-existence of any middle ground between pro-life (the anti-abortionists) and pro-choice (a woman's right to choose what to do with her body).

Is abortion exclusively: A moral issue? A legal issue? A social issue? A religious issue? A mixture?

And who ultimately decides?

However, there may be a "solution" that has some measure of appeal to both sides.

It should appeal to the conservatives because it follows a major point of their expressed values, individual responsibility. And it appeals to the liberals because it doesn't require the woman to shoulder the entire burden of childbirth and child-rearing. In fact, the burden is shared equally.

The proposed solution would require legislation by the states. We know red states are outlawing abortion—some with no exceptions, others with varying degrees of exceptions, such as in cases where the mother's health is jeopardized. Blue states, however, are generally following Roe v. Wade.

Here is the proposal. Consider what the several states' reactions might be.

Currently, the average cost to raise a child from birth to age 21 is $233,610.

Simply pass a law that splits this financial burden 50-50 between both parents.

If a birth father refuses to acknowledge paternity, a court order requiring him to take a paternity test should be mandated. There's enough out there in DNA land to take care of such refusal.

To assure the birth parents share the financial burden (assuming no adoption or foster home placement, or similar type of placement that removes the birth parents from further legal responsibility for the child), repeal all exemptions from garnishment and property seizure laws.

Whatever earnings either parent makes would be subject to garnishment of wages to meet the financial obligation from birth to adulthood. (If the child is still in college at age 21, the cost to graduation would be equally shared.) Exemptions from garnishment allow the person to keep a sum for himself/herself before meeting whatever obligations the garnishment serves. Under this proposed law, however, the first priority of the person's income would be to the child.

This would all be fleshed out in court, in the same manner as property is divided in a family law dissolution of marriage case.

With regard to seizure of property, under current law, certain items are exempt from seizure and sale to satisfy a judgment--a person's primary residence, primary vehicle, etc. For the purpose of dealing with this particular subject, these exemptions would be eliminated. Again, the top priority would be the child. And again, the court would superintend the seizure, sale and disposition of proceeds for the raising of the child.

If, for example, a court, after considering all relevant matters regarding income of both parents, and their needs and possessions, the judge were to require each parent to pay a set sum for the raising of the child each month or each quarter, that amount would be given top priority over the financial and related needs of the birth parents.

There may be those who consider such a law draconian; but how draconian is it to prevent a woman from exercising her free choice? And how draconian is it to those who believe abortion is the unlawful taking of life?

Notice the Supreme Court didn't outlaw abortion; it just left the matter to the states. Here is a proposal that is faithful to the Court's decision.

And if both parents knew early on that if they bring a child into the world, deliberately or by accident (unplanned), they will be held fully and equally accountable, perhaps they will think twice or be more careful in their relationship.

I don't see anything wrong with that.

WHO IS RESPONSIBLE FOR SOCIAL SECURITY AND PENSIONS, AND WHO WANTS TO SEE THEIR CURTAILMENT OR DEMISE?

As we move toward another election cycle, it is important to consider our nation's history over the past 100 years and decide which political party was responsible for certain actions, both harmful and helpful.

The Great Depression-- the Great Depression was caused largely by the stock market crash of 1929; the collapse of world trade due to ill-conceived tariffs; timid government policies; bank failures and panics; and the collapse of the money supply.

During the period from 1921 and leading up the 1929 crash, Republicans controlled both houses of Congress and the White House, with Warren Harding, Calvin Coolidge and Herbert Hoover as president.

To aggressively deal with the most devastating economic crisis in our nation's history, the Democrat Party focused on the "three-legged stool;" the description of the three common sources of retirement income: Social Security, pensions, and personal savings.

Social Security--This law provided for unemployment insurance, old-age insurance, and means-tested welfare programs. The Great Depression was clearly a catalyst for the Social Security Act of 1935, and some of its provisions—notably the means-tested programs—were intended to offer immediate relief to families.

Social insurance, as conceived by President Roosevelt, would address the permanent problem of economic security for the elderly by creating a work-related, contributory system in which workers would provide for their own future economic security through taxes paid while employed.

Social Security played a large role in helping the country to reconstruct and recover from the hardships of living during the Great Depression.

Today, approximately 69 million Americans receive Social Security. The party split is about even, so roughly 34 million Republicans receive social security checks.

Thus, Republicans benefit from a program started by the Democrats in response to the economic meltdown of the late 1920s.

The first present to tax Social Security was Ronald Reagan in 1984. Over the years, Republicans have repeatedly discussed the importance of reducing federal entitlement programs to manage the federal deficit. The largest federal entitlement programs are Social Security, comprising about 23% of federal spending, and Medicare/Medicaid/ healthcare subsidies, comprising about 25% of federal spending. In fact, over the years, Republican law makers have introduced bills that reduce Social Security's funding deficit primarily by cutting benefits.

Donald Trump has stated that he wants to reduce or eliminate payroll taxes that support Social Security. I wonder if the 34 million Republicans currently on Social Security know this.

Pensions--Up until the 1980s and Reagan Administration, defined-benefit pensions were the most popular retirement plan offered by employers. Today, only 15% of private-sector workers have access to one, according to the March 2021 National Compensation Survey from the Bureau of Labor Statistics

Since the 1980s, 401(k) accounts have effectively replaced pensions to become one of the most popular retirement plans for American workers

In 2020, there were about 600,000 401(k) plans, with approximately 60 million Americans participating in them.

Pensions offer greater stability than 401(k) plans. With a pension, a pensioner is guaranteed a fixed monthly payment every month following retirement. Because it's a fixed amount, the pensioner is able to budget based on steady payments from the combination of a fixed pension and Social Security benefits.

A 401(k) is less stable, subject to the vagaries of the stock market. During the Great Recession of 2008—the last year of the Bush II Administration--major U.S. equity indexes were sharply negative, with the S&P 500 Index losing 37.0 percent for the year, which translated into corresponding losses in 401(k) retirement plan assets.

A separate survey conducted by the Pension Rights Center found that 66 percent of retirees currently receive income from these 401k-types of financial assets. Less than one-third (31%) of Americans are retiring with a defined benefit pension plan today.

From the employee's perspective, the beauty of a defined-benefit plan is that the employer funds the plan while the employee reaps the rewards upon retirement. Not only do employees get to keep and spend all the money they earn in their paychecks, but they can also easily predict how much money they will receive each month during retirement because payouts from a defined-benefit plan are based on a set formula.

From an employer's perspective, defined-benefit plans are an ongoing liability. Funding for the plans must come from corporate earnings, and this has a direct impact on profits. A drag on profits can weaken a company's ability to compete. Switching to a defined-contribution plan such as a 401(k), which is mainly funded by employee contributions, saves a significant amount of money.

Over the last few decades, private-sector companies increasingly stopped funding their traditional pension plans, which is known as a freeze. A freeze is the first step toward the elimination of the plan.

Corporate America has defended these moves on the grounds that the government has made moves to force companies to fully fund their pension plans. The Pension Protection Act of 2006, for example, mandated stricter funding requirements to help ensure that employees get paid benefits.

But companies haven't always fully funded the plans. All too often, the money hasn't been there when it's needed, and the government has been forced to bail out the plans. This path has been taken by several airlines and a contingent of steelmakers over the years, all of which filed for bankruptcy and shifted the responsibility for their retirement plan obligations onto the U.S. government. The government, in turn, shifted the burden to taxpayers.

Defined-benefit pension plans are still somewhat common in the public sector, especially for those who work in the government.

So what does the end of defined-benefits plans mean for employees? The entire scenario is bad news. Unlike a defined-benefit plan, where employees know exactly what their benefits will be in retirement, the only certainty in a defined-contribution plan is the amount that the employee contributes. Many employers also offer matching contributions.

After the money hits the account, it's up to the employee to choose how it's invested (typically from a menu of mutual funds) and the vagaries of the stock market to determine the ultimate outcome. Maybe the markets will go up, and maybe they won't.

On the other hand, many employees who were relying on their employer-funded plans were left to fend for themselves when their employers failed to fund the plans. Similarly, many employees were left in a bind when their employers terminated defined-benefit plans or downsized their staff, giving the workers a one-time, lump-sum payout instead of a steady income stream.

Make no mistake about it: corporate America--Big Business--has been the driving force in ending defined-benefit pensions in exchange for plans that require investments that are subject to market influences. And we know which political party is more favorably disposed toward Big Business, and which party Big Business favors.

The information above is culled from many sources. It is admittedly difficult, if not impossible, to capture the details and nuances of these subjects in a shot narrative. What is important, however, is that the electorate become aware of our economic history by using what's here as a springboard to reading as many sources as possible to get a complete picture of what was, what is now, and what the future portends, depending on the choices we make at the polls.

WHAT IS AUTHORITARIANISM; WHAT DOES THE AUTHORITARIAN LIKE AND DISLIKE?

Authoritarianism is characterized by highly concentrated and centralized government power maintained by political repression and the exclusion of potential challengers. It uses political parties and mass organizations to mobilize people around the goals of the leader.

Both totalitarianism and authoritarianism discourage individual freedom of thought and action. Totalitarianism attempts to do this by asserting total control over the lives of its citizens, whereas authoritarianism prefers the blind submission of its citizens to authority.

Authoritarian leadership means that the leader has full power. Authoritarian leaders tell groups what to do and expect group members to execute; they are more likely to disregard the good ideas of others, believing they are superior to everyone else. The style can also inspire resentment and stress.

While benevolent authoritarian leaders might achieve some good results, others may cause major harm. The Kim family of North Korea is an extreme case of authoritarian leadership. In North Korea, senior advisers are terrified of Kim-Jong Un with good reason. Instead of honest advice, these men offer useless flattery. Unchecked, an authoritarian leader can prove disastrous. Other examples of what can only be described charitably as less than benevolent authoritarian leaders include Russia's Putin and China's Xi. History is replete with examples of authoritarian/despots, most notably Hitler, Mussolini, Pol Pot, Idi Amin, and their kind.

Authoritarian leaders want people who offer praise, genuflect to his word, not question or disagree with him, and profess unyielding loyalty.

For the authoritarian, control is essential. He doesn't like a free press because he must not be made to appear weak, and asking questions that make him uncomfortable translates to showing weakness. Further, facing pointed questions invokes accountability; the authoritarian doesn't feel the need to explain his actions.

The authoritarian must never be put in a position of having to justify what he says or does. Blind acceptance is essential to authoritarian control. His definition of a free press is one that agrees with him and shows him in a favorable light at all times.

The authoritarian opposes academic freedom, unless he can define it to mean instruction that conforms to his ideology and paints him in a positive light. He will ban any instruction or teaching that challenges his ideology or portrays him and his supporters in a less than favorable light.

He opposes teaching history warts and all. He doesn't want people to learn the harsh lessons history teaches in part because that might force him to explain his actions in historical perspective, and explanations cut against blind loyalty. He will attempt to re-write history and whitewash or eliminate matters that he finds uncomfortable or make him and his supporters feel some sense of guilt. Objectivity is anathema to the authoritarian unless he can define what objectivity means to suits his needs.

He rejects science and the scientific method because they teach people to think independently, using critical thinking skills. He demands—and must have--steadfast loyalty and adherence to his every word. Anything, including critical thinking skills, that smacks of possible resistance to the authoritarian's word is not permitted and will subject critics to punishment.

Authoritarian leaders want people to suspend notions of reality and accept the authoritarian's version of events, conditions and circumstances. The old adage "Who are you going to believe, me or your lying eyes" is very much a part of the authoritarian leader's playbook.

Fear is a vital component of the authoritarian playbook. He thrives on an "us against them" mentality, and uses carefully chosen words and phrases the purpose of which is to conjure up in the mind of the audience anger, resentment and rage against "them." Fear is an essential element of control.

Of course, for the authoritarian leader to be successful, he must loyal followers who accept him, his words and deeds without reservation or hesitation. In this light, Groupthink, the practice of thinking or making decisions as a group in a way that discourages creativity or individual responsibility, is essential to the authoritarian.

A study reported in Politico found that "authoritarians are more likely to agree that our country should be governed by a strong leader who doesn't have to bother with Congress or elections. They are more likely to support limiting the freedom of the press and agree that the media is the enemy of the people rather than a valuable independent institution. They are also more likely to think the president should have the power to limit the voice and vote of opposition parties, while believing that those who disagree with them are a threat to our country—a concerning trend as we head to the polls this year.

American authoritarians fear diversity. They are more likely to agree that increasing racial, religious and ethnic diversity is a clear and present threat to national security. They are more fearful of people of other races, and agree with the statement that 'sometimes other groups must be kept in their place.'" (This quote comes from George Orwell's "1984.")

See anything familiar here?

CONSERVATIVE GURU RUPERT MURDOCH HAS HAD ENOUGH OF TRUMP

Donald Trump has proven to be too much baggage for conservative Rupert Murdoch and his New York Post. Murdoch has declared Trump "unworthy to be president again." This is the former head of "fair and balanced" FOX News finally dumping Trump. Wow!

Of course, it took criminal conduct leading up to and including January 6 to finally get Murdoch's attention, but at least he, and more temperate conservatives, have had enough of Trump. The savvy Murdoch should have seen what was coming years ago, but perhaps "better late than never' is appropriate here.

Trump's longtime flag carrier, Steve Bannon, has attacked Murdoch in the past. And Trump continues to engage in a pity party, moaning about being the most persecuted president in American history. That this might because he's the most corrupt president in American history doesn't register on his radar screen--or that of his unwavering loyalists.

Perhaps between now and the November elections and beyond, more and more with traditional conservative values (whatever they may be in actual practice, not buzzwords) will turn against Trump, and then turn on one another. You can bet the Pence forces and the DeSantis forces are sharpening their knives (metaphorically, of course) – and no doubt others with visions of the White House dancing in their heads (Abbott, Hawley, etc.) are doing likewise.

This should make for interesting times over the next several months, especially when the House select committee's final report on January 6 is released and names names, pictures included. Some of those names may be among those with visions of sugarplums dancing in their heads. And then there's the Department of Justice and the several federal prosecutors who have yet to chime in. You can bet they will. Even for diehard conservatives, there is a point at which enough is enough.

TRUMP WANTS TO ELIMINATE THE FEDERAL CIVIL SERVICE SYSTEM; ANOTHER ATTACK ON DEMOCRACY

Author/historian Heather Cox Richardson paints a stark picture should Donald Trump return to the White House. Trump wants to scrap the federal civil service system and replace it with appointed cronies and those with unyielding loyalty to him. As Richardson notes: "The idea of reducing our professional civil service to those who offer loyalty to a single leader is yet another fundamental attack on democracy."

Conservatives believe they are of superior intelligence, firmly believing that liberals are incapable of logical, rational thinking that conservatives are known for. Remember, however, that it wasn't the Democrats who bought Trump's Big Lie; it wasn't the Democrats who stormed the capital, and it isn't the Democrats who endorse QAnon conspiracy theories or support white supremacists and white nationalists and their politics of racism and hate. Moreover, we know that many Republicans--including his own appointees--told Trump the truth that he lost the election--and Trump knew that he lost--yet he continued to lie about it.

To this day, he still pushes his Big lie, and his blind loyalists and supporters still believe in him. And they further believe the attack on the capital was just good people engaging in legitimate political discourse. This alone doesn't demonstrate superior intelligence they claim they possess.

He wants to scrap the civil service system with this example of intelligence. To him, intelligence doesn't matter at all; loyalty does.

TRUMP'S LOYALISTS WANT AMERICA TO BECOME CHRISTIAN NATIONALISTS

Here is a headline that should send chills up and down the spine:

Rep. Marjorie Taylor Greene Says GOP 'Should Be Christian Nationalists' Party.'

The Republican Party's primary focus this year should be on making the political party one of Christian nationalism, Rep. Marjorie Taylor Greene (R-Ga.) said Saturday.

"We need to be the party of nationalism and I'm a Christian, and I say it proudly, we should be Christian nationalists," she said in an interview with the conservative Next News Network while attending the Turning Point USA Student Action Summit in Florida.

Does she have a clue what she's talking about? Does she and those who support her even care about the consequences of such a statement to our Democracy?

According to a CNN article, the January 6 "insurrection marked the first time many Americans realized our nation is facing a burgeoning White Christian nationalist movement. This movement uses Christian language to cloak sexism and hostility to Black people and non-White immigrants in its quest to create a White Christian America.

A report from a team of clergy, scholars and advocates — sponsored by two groups that advocate for the separation of church and state — concluded that this ideology was used to "bolster, justify and intensify" the attack on the nation's Capital.

Much of the House January 6 committee's focus so far has been on right-wing extremist groups. But there are plenty of other Americans who have adopted teachings of the White Christian nationalists who stormed the Capitol — often without knowing it, scholars, historians, sociologists and clergy say.

White Christian nationalist beliefs have infiltrated the religious mainstream so thoroughly that virtually any conservative Christian pastor who tries to challenge its ideology risks their career, says Kristin Kobes Du Mez, author of the New York Times bestseller, 'Jesus and John Wayne: How White Evangelicals Corrupted a Faith and Fractured a Nation.'

These ideas are so widespread that any individual pastor or Christian leader who tries to turn the tide and say, 'Let's look again at Jesus and scripture,' are going to be tossed aside,' she says.

The ideas are also insidious because many sound like expressions of Christian piety or harmless references to US history. But White Christian nationalists interpret these ideas in ways that are potentially violent and heretical. Their movement is not only anti-democratic, it contradicts the life and teachings of Jesus, some clergy, scholars and historians say."

Greene is clearly advocating the destruction of the wall separating church and state. She is certainly not alone. Rep. Lauren Boebert (R.Colo.) says she is "tired" of separation between church and state: "The church is supposed to direct the government." They have allies in Congress and the Supreme Court who believe in the elimination of historical church-state separation.

This is not intelligence; this is destructive of our form of government. It is sheer lunacy. The questions that must be asked are: Is this what conservatives want America to be? Do they want America to become a theocracy, like so many Middle East countries? Is this the level of intelligence we want from our government leaders?

AMERICA'S GREATEST THREAT IS FROM WITHIN

A group of Nazi demonstrators gathered outside the Tampa Convention Center the other day. The center was playing host to the conservative Turning Point USA Student Action Summit. Photos taken of the group showed them waving posters with anti-Semitic imagery, such as swastikas and Nazi flags, along with the Florida state flag and a poster showing Florida Gov. Ron DeSantis' face.

DeSantis had a chance to condemn the actions of Nazi demonstrators earlier this year. In January, following Nazi demonstrations that took place near Orlando, DeSantis lashed out at those who called on him to condemn these demonstrations, accusing his political opponents of trying to "smear me as if I had something to do with it."

Rep. Lauren Boebert (R.Colo.) says she is "tired" of separation between church and state: "The church is supposed to direct the government."

Rep. Marjorie Taylor Greene (R. Georgia) says the Republican Party "Should Be Christian Nationalists' Party."

Judging from the crowds Boebert, Greene and others of a similar mind are drawing at rallies and conventions, this line of thinking is certainly not isolated. Far from it.

Increasingly, members of the media, academics and others are using the term "Christian nationalism" and "white Christian nationalism" to describe a political movement that seeks to topple church-state separation and declare America a "Christian nation" – with "Christian" in this case being far to the right and supremely fundamentalist. This fits Boebert's and Greene's goals—and again we know they are certainly not alone.

The general consensus is that white nationalist groups espouse white supremacist or white separatist ideologies, often focusing on the alleged inferiority of nonwhites. Groups listed in a variety of other categories—Ku Klux

Klan, neo-Confederate, neo-Nazi, racist skinhead and Christian Identity—could also be fairly described as white nationalist.

In January, DeSantis had a chance to condemn what these demonstrators stand for. Instead, he tried to blame his political opponents from blaming him for their actions. This is classic deflection; he wasn't being blamed, but his failure to condemn them could legitimately be viewed as support or endorsement by silence.

We expect our elected leaders to (among other duties) support the constitution, adhere to the rule of law, and oppose any enemy, foreign or domestic. Domestic.

There should be a national outcry over the unmistakable message the above brief narrative sends; so far, it has been met mostly with silence.

We have been a democratic republic for almost 250 years. What is to become of our country if what is set out above becomes mainstream? One thing is certain: silence or timidity is not a legitimate response to what our federal government has said is the greatest threat to our nation.

INDOCTRINATON AND BRAINWASHING

Both words are being tossed around as weapons to justify one's beliefs while castigating others. They have become a form of epithets that are supposed to explain what the "other side" is suffering from. However, what is missing is a basic understanding of what these words actually mean. It is admittedly impossible to discuss the depth of meaning of these words. Books have been written about both words, their meanings, applications, etc.

In this light, here are some basic definitions and examples of both words. The next time you hear or see them, you will have some idea what the speaker or writer is talking about—assuming they know.

Indoctrination means "to imbue with a usually partisan or sectarian opinion, point of view, or principle; to instruct especially in fundamentals or rudiments."

Examples of indoctrination "include hiding facts, disparaging student opinions, or rejecting any ideas that contradict the teacher's beliefs. Indoctrination is a means of forcing, brainwashing, or imposing desired ideologies without open discussion."

Indoctrination techniques include the use of propaganda, brainwashing, censorship and other restrictions on freedom of expression and information, advertising, angled phrasing and contents of government and official information, with monopoly of the media."

Brainwashing is "a forcible indoctrination to induce someone to give up basic political, social, or religious beliefs and attitudes and to accept contrasting regimented ideas; persuasion by propaganda or salesmanship.

Brainwashing is commonly associated with cults and abuse. A cult leader might, for example, present a warm and friendly disposition to gain a person's trust, then slowly break down the person by calling him or her names, forcing him or her to work, and engaging in other forms of abuse.

Common features of brainwashing include isolation, humiliation, accusation, and unpredictable attacks.

Someone who is brainwashed rarely questions things that they're told by their leader or the person they look up to, and they often don't have their own opinions. Helping someone who's brainwashed can be challenging, and it can take a long time since their ideas are deeply rooted in their mind.

In psychology, the study of brainwashing, often referred to as thought reform, falls into the sphere of "social influence." Social influence happens every minute of every day. It's the collection of ways in which people can change other people's attitudes, beliefs and behaviors. For instance, the compliance method aims to produce a change in a person's behavior and is not concerned with his attitudes or beliefs. It's the "Just do it" approach. Persuasion, on the other hand, aims for a change in attitude, or "Do it because it'll make you feel good/happy/healthy/successful." The education method (which is called the "propaganda method" when you don't believe in what's being taught) goes for the social-influence gold, trying to affect a change in the person's beliefs, along the lines of "Do it because you know it's the right thing to do." Brainwashing is a severe form of social influence that combines all of these approaches to cause changes in someone's way of thinking without that person's consent and often against his will."

Four signs of a brainwashed person are: They're no longer themselves; they've turned into someone else. They are obsessed with their new beliefs, group, and the group leader; they can't stop talking about these. They have a strong attachment to their new beliefs. They follow the group leader unthinkingly, sometimes to their own detriment.

Indoctrination and brainwashing are near synonyms; however, indoctrination is a much older (17th century) word which originally merely meant "teach," applied mainly to the teaching of religion; brainwashing as a word did not appear until the 1950s." At that time, brainwashing was used to describe how the Chinese government appeared to make people cooperate with them. Research into the concept also looked at Nazi Germany, at some criminal cases in the United States, and at the actions of human traffickers. In the late 1960s and 1970s, there was considerable scientific and legal debate about its use in the conversion of people to groups that are considered to be cults.

There is a difference between education and brainwashing. "Education informs learners about the facts around them and helps them become critical thinkers. In contrast, brainwashing provides learners with heavily biased information that leads to one predetermined conclusion."

THE PSYCHOLOGICAL PRICE WE PAY FOR MASS SHOOTINGS

Some say these mass shootings are the price we pay for our freedoms. I don't accept such a cavalier, throw-up-the-arms-in-despair attitude. It's the attitude of the weak-minded.

Fear can debilitate; it can paralyze. My question is how free can one be if he/she thinks about this possibility each time he/she walks into a mall, a supermarket or shopping center, place of worship, or even a barber shop or beauty salon, a gym or health club, and any other place where people congregate?

It is of no value to simply say "well, just try not to think about it." Just trying to avoid thinking about it means you're thinking about it. Sort of a "damned if you do, damned if you don't" dilemma. When one is fearful, one isn't free.

One of Franklin Roosevelt's "Four Freedoms" was "Freedom from Fear." Although he was talking about worldwide disarmament to avoid the prospect of World War III, living in fear of some form of domestic violence by mass shootings is just as debilitating; perhaps even more so because this type of fear is over something that can happen in a nearby mall, school, church, etc. Maybe even the ones you visit.

HATRIOT AND HATRIOTISM

Here's a word that might appear unfamiliar; it was to me until just the other day. That word is hatriot. A hatriot is defined as "a reactionary political conservative who criticizes liberal or progressive stances as unpatriotic." Another definition is "anyone who loudly and publicly exhibits hatred against a person or race or nation or religion and believes that they are serving the national interest."

Hatriots and hatriotism were on full display on America's latest day of infamy, January 6 of last year, when armed with weapons and firmly convinced of the Big Lie that they swallowed hook, line and sinker, they attacked our nation's capital. The hatriots' acts of sedition involved their assault of over 140 law enforcement officers and threats against the lives of then-Vice President Mike Pence and several members of Congress. Videos of that insurrection showed them using the American Flag as a weapon to beat law enforcement officers.

Before the attack that day, they were told they are patriots and that they needed to take back their country. After more than three hours of a relentless attack on the capital, they were told that they are loved. Think about that: using the American Flag to beat those whose duty it is to uphold law and order, and then being told that they are loved!

To this day, there are tens of millions who continue to see nothing out of line or strange about what happened before and during January 6. The harsh truth of the events leading up to and including that day are being disclosed to the American public by the House select committee investigating the attack. Although the evidence is coming from Republicans, including those who were in Donald Trump's White House, hatriots continue to deny this reality in favor of what they are being fed by those they worship.

While they can deny and deflect, the reality is that it wasn't the Democrats who whipped up a mob frenzy on January 6 with a Big Lie of election rigging. It wasn't the Democrats who attacked the capital and injured over 140 law enforcement officers. And it isn't the Democrats who offered incriminating evidence to the House committee and the American people of criminal conduct committed by former President Trump and his allies.

And yet despite the clear evidence, there are certain elements, including the hatriots, who have the unmitigated gall to accuse Democrats—as well as others, including members of the Republican Party--of being indoctrinated and brainwashed. The short of it is they make the same charge against anyone who dares to challenge Trump and his loyalists.

Nevertheless, hatriots continue to wave the American Flag, misquote the Bible and believe violence is the answer. What they can't do is fool the vast majority of Americans who see who the real patriots are: those who are holding the rioters accountable, those who are on the House committee seeking to uncover the truth about January 6, and those who testified—and will testify--under oath offering damning evidence about the gravest domestic threat to our Democracy in our nation's history. And everyone else who rejects hatriots and hatriotism.

NO PERSON IS ABOVE THE LAW: THERE IS NO FUNCTIONAL EQUIVALENCY BETWEEN HUNTER BIDEN AND DONALD TRUMP

No person is above the law. Merrick Garland is just the latest attorney general to speak these words. America is a nation of laws, not of men. So, it's appropriate to investigate possible or potential criminal conduct regardless of race, creed, ethnicity, etc.--or political persuasion.

Investigating Hunter Biden for financial irregularities that might be criminal is certainly appropriate. But so is investigating Donald Trump and his allies for possible criminal conduct arising out of January 6.

There are people who believe that Hunter Biden allows for explaining away or simply ignoring what Donald Trump and his cohorts did. One thing is certain: pointing out the actions of one doesn't explain or justify the other. A mass shooting is not the functional equivalent of a burglary. Both are crimes and must be treated as such. Both have penalties and must be meted out according to the law. But to believe that someone else's crooked behavior allows forgiveness for, excuses, or is equal to another's crooked behavior is simply not how the American justice system operates. And it must never be allowed to function that way if Democracy is to survive.

AUTOMOBILES VS. ASSAULT WEAPONS: A FLAWED, ILLOGICAL ANALOGY

Whenever the subject of banning assault weapons comes up, someone predictably asks why automobiles aren't banned, since more people are killed by automobiles than by assault weapons.

This argument suffers from the illogical premise called the false equivalence.

It goes something like this: "We can't ban guns just because they can be used to hurt people. After all, cars can be used to hurt people, so if we ban guns then we would have to ban cars too!" This argument is fallacious because it draws a false equivalence between guns and cars based simply on the fact that they can be used to hurt people.

Here is an explanation of this flawed, illogical analogy.

An automobile is not a weapon; an assault weapon is. That's why it's called an assault weapon.

The main purpose of an automobile is to provide transportation. Try going to work, shopping, sports events, vacation, etc. without one. An automobile is defined as "a road vehicle, typically with four wheels, designed primarily for passenger transportation and commonly powered by an internal combustion engine or electric motor and able to carry a small number of people." A car that is idle--parked on the street or in the garage--is not being used for that overriding purpose. Unless a person is a collector who uses his/her automobile for display (and the collector most likely will need some form of transportation to get the collector's item to its show destination and back home), an auto's intended purpose is transportation.

The main purpose of an assault weapon is to shoot; to eject bullets. It is the same purpose behind every firearm. The Constitution uses the phrase "bear arms." That refers to "weapons and ammunition; armaments;" specifically, "to carry or be equipped with weapons."

A firearm is defined as "any weapon (including a starter gun) which will or is designed to or may readily be converted to expel a projectile by the action of an explosive." Of course, there are collectors who display their weapons in the same manner as automobiles. (It is much easier to get the firearms to exhibitions than automobiles, however.) A firearm on the shelf, above a fireplace or in one's pocket or holster is not being used for its intended purpose. Without question, however, a firearm's salient purpose as demonstrated by these definitions, is to shoot.

In 2021, there were 42,915 deaths across America that involved the use of an automobile. The 12 major causes of automobile-related deaths are, in order: speeding, driving while under the influence, veering into another lane, failure to yield, distracted driving, careless driving, overcorrecting, failure to obey signals, reckless driving, swerving to avoid, weather, and drowsiness. Approximately 31% of all automobile-related deaths involve alcohol and/or drugs.

The common denominator underlying automobile deaths is an irresponsible driver. Responsible drivers don't drive while under the influence, fail to obey signals, drive recklessly or carelessly, drive while using cellphones or are otherwise distracted, excessively exceed posted speed limits, etc.

The number of deaths caused by mass shootings is far less. A mass shooting is usually defined as one involving four or more people, excluding the shooter. In 2021, 705 were killed in mass shootings. But all that is needed for a mass shooting is a place where people congregate, a lone gunman who is either mentally ill or snaps, and relatively easy access to a weapon of mass murder, an assault weapon.

I am not referring to the law-abiding citizen or the responsible gun owner. (Although whether the law-abiding citizen or responsible gun owner needs an assault weapon for self-defense is another matter.) However, how many responsible owners leave their firearms where a troubled family member, relative, neighbor or visitor can easily access it? The sad fact is someone's inadvertence or perhaps a single act of negligence can lead to a horrific crime. We have had instances of mass shootings under some of these scenarios, particularly involving a family member.

As previously noted, mass shooting killings are not nearly as frequent as automobile-related fatalities. But I doubt there are many drivers who get behind the wheel with the deliberate intent in mind to mow down as many pedestrians as he can. The same can't be said about those who get their hands on an assault weapon, perhaps post their feelings and emotions on various websites or in their notes or dairies, and carry out their intent in places where people congregate.

Besides, numbers are of no significance to family and friends of those whose lives are lost to a mass shooter.

No doubt someone will look at the percentage of DUI deaths and make the same claim for banning alcohol or drugs. Such an argument also suffers from a false equivalency. Ask what the main purpose of alcohol is. And the same with drugs. It is not to kill or maim.

The irresponsible automobile driver is not as lethal as the crazed wielder of an assault weapon. I'm not aware of anyone who has driven an automobile into a church, school, mall, movie theater, gym, etc., and massacred people.

Another argument made in opposition to banning assault weapons is that it is the first step toward confiscation of other weapons. This is the domino theory approach; that is, knocking one domino into others will cause them to fall, too. Although the domino theory is flawed because the occurrence of one part doesn't mean another will occur, the more significant flaw here is that the Second Amendment bars such a scenario. The Heller case makes abundantly clear that while there is a constitutional right to bear arms, Congress can ban certain weapons of war, and can limit possession in certain circumstances. The scope of the Second Amendment is yet to be fully fleshed out; however, the notion that banning assault weapons means eventual confiscation or banning of weapons already protected by that amendment is bogus.

The bottom line: An automobile is not a weapon. Alcohol and drugs are not weapons. There isn't a single definition that describes any of these as a weapon. An assault weapon is a weapon.

Whatever argument one wants to make in support of sale, possession and use of assault weapons, don't use the one about automobiles.

DEMOCRACY IS FACING A CRISIS OF CONFIDENCE: PUBLIC TRUST IN GOVERNMENT IS DECLINING

It is said we are a government of laws, not of men. Yet it is people who pass laws; it is people who implement those laws; and it is people who decide what the laws means, with the Supreme Court having the final say of what the Constitution means.

We elect our representatives to pass laws; we elect representatives to implement those law either directly or through appointed officials, who are generally confirmed by elected representatives. And their decisions are subject to review by justices and judges who reach office by appointment and confirmation or through a form of merit selection and retention. At least, this is the way the system is designed to function.

It has always been this way in America because government functioned with "the consent of the governed."

And therein lies the heart of our current crisis. Public trust in government is declining; this portends great danger for the survival of our democratic republic. When discontent is persistent, a vacuum is created. It's the prospect of what might fill that vacuum that should give us pause.

Historically, even when confidence in the Congress and presidency was low, public confidence in the Supreme Court remained relatively high and stable. Even after the furor over the 2000 presidential election, once emotions cooled, the "consent of the governed" prevailed.

Popular support for the Supreme Court, however, has taken a significant hit, reaching an historic low.

According to the most recent Gallup poll, Americans' confidence in the court has dropped sharply over the past year and reached a new low in the survey's nearly 50-year trend. According to this poll, 25% of adults say they have "a great deal" or "quite a lot" of confidence in the Supreme Court, down from 36% a year ago and five percentage points lower than the previous low recorded in 2014.

In September 2021, "Gallup found the Supreme Court's job approval rating at a new low and public trust in the judicial branch of the federal government down sharply The prior low in Supreme Court confidence was 30% in 2014, which was also the year when confidence in major U.S. institutions in general hit a low point, averaging 31%.

Public confidence in the Supreme Court has been lower over the past 16 years than it was before. Between 1973 and 2006, an average of 47% of adults were confident in the Court. During this 33-year period, no fewer than four in 10 Americans expressed high confidence in the court in any survey, apart from a 39% reading in October 1991 taken during the Clarence Thomas confirmation hearings.

Since 2006, confidence has averaged 35% and has not exceeded 40% in any survey.

This poll recognizes that its numbers might well be driven at least in part by the brouhaha over the recently released abortion decision; however, the poll also notes an historic trend, and that is what should be troubling for our nation.

Another poll, this one by Pew Research Center, is equally troubling.

Overall, public trust in government remains low, as it has for much of the 21st century. Only two-in-ten Americans say they trust the government in Washington to do what is right "just about always" (2%) or "most of the time" (19%). Trust in the government has declined somewhat since last year, when 24% said they could trust the government at least most of the time. Sixty-five percent say most political candidates run for office 'to serve their own personal interests'

"When the National Election Study began asking about trust in government in 1958, about three-quarters of Americans trusted the federal government to do the right thing almost always or most of the time. Trust in government began eroding during the 1960s, amid the escalation of the Vietnam War, and the decline continued in the 1970s with the Watergate scandal and worsening economic struggles. Confidence in government recovered in the mid-1980s before falling again in the mid-1990s. But as the economy grew in the late 1990s, so too did confidence in government. Public trust reached a three-decade high shortly after the 9/11 terrorist attacks, but declined quickly thereafter. Since 2007, the shares saying they can trust the government always or most of the time has not surpassed 30%.

Today, 29% of Democrats and Democratic-leaning independents say they trust government just about always or most of the time, compared with 9% of Republicans and Republican-leaners. Democrats report slightly less trust in the federal government today than a year ago; there has been no change in the views of Republicans."

Historically, trust in government is higher among members of the party that controls the presidency. But even in those cases, trust is low overall. Since the 1970s, trust in government has been consistently higher among members of the party that controls the White House than among the opposition party. Republicans have often been more reactive than Democrats to changes in political leadership, with Republicans expressing much lower levels of trust during Democratic presidencies; Democrats' attitudes have tended to be somewhat more consistent, regardless of which party controls the White House. However, the GOP and Democratic shifts in attitudes between the end of the Trump presidency and the early Biden administration were roughly the same magnitude.

People generally want to put their faith and trust in their government. But when they can't, won't or don't do that, where do they turn, and who do they turn to?

HUNTER BIDEN AND DONALD TRUMP: ANOTHER FALSE EQUIVALENCE, ANOTHER ILLOGICAL ARGUMENT

Some Republicans are chomping at the bit for criminal charges to be brought against Hunter Biden because he happens to be President Joe Biden's son. These party faithful believe that bringing charges against Biden somehow equates with the criminal charges that former President Trump may face down the road.

This argument suffers from the illogical premise called the false equivalence.

False equivalence is a fallacy in which an equivalence is drawn between two subjects based on flawed or false reasoning. This fallacy is categorized as a fallacy of inconsistency. Here, it is simply inconsistent to equate Hunter Biden with Donald Trump. The status of both, and the seriousness of the crimes they may face, are worlds apart.

The other day, I discussed the illogic behind equating guns with cars. It went like this: “We can’t ban guns just because they can be used to hurt people. After all, cars can be used to hurt people, so if we ban guns then we would have to ban cars too!” I said this argument is fallacious because it draws a false equivalence between guns and cars based simply on the fact that they can be used to hurt people. There is no equivalence between the main purposes of guns and cars.

It is no different between trying to draw an equivalence between Hunter Biden and Donald Trump.

Hunter Biden is a private citizen. Donald Trump is a former President of the United States. Biden’s criminal exposure stems from his status as a private citizen. Trump’s criminal exposure stems from his conduct as the highest elected official in America, bound by his oath to “preserve, protect and defend the Constitution of the United States” and bound by the Constitution itself to “take care that the Laws be faithfully executed.” Hunter Biden took no such oath, and is not bound by the words that bound Donald Trump during his term in the White House.

For Biden, the legal issues are tax law violations, money laundering, acting as an unregistered foreign lobbyist, and prostitution for illegally bringing minors across state lines. He is currently under investigation by the Department of Justice and a federal grand jury in Delaware.

For Trump, the legal issues are sedition, inciting a riot, obstruction of justice, witness tampering, conspiracy to commit these offenses, dereliction of duty, conspiracy to defraud the United States and bribery. Except for witness tampering, these crimes arise out of Trump's actions, or failure to act when bound by duty, while president; there may be others, depending on additional evidence presented by Republican witnesses to the House select committee on January 6's capital riot. He is currently under investigation by the Department of Justice. And there are state charges possibly arising out of election tampering in Georgia. Trump also faces pre-presidency charges involving financial irregularities in New York. There may also be other federal and state investigations that haven't yet been publicized.

Conspiracy to defraud the United States criminalizes any effort by two or more people to interfere with governmental functions "by deceit, craft or trickery." In addition to Trump's efforts to pressure his Vice President, Mike Pence, to upend the Electoral College vote, his attempts to convince state election officials, the public and members of Congress that the 2020 election was stolen, even though several of his allies told him there was no evidence of fraud, are cited as a basis for this charge.

The witness tampering issue involves actions Trump took during the House select committee hearings.

The bribery issue arises out of Trump's phone call to Ukraine President Zelensky during his failed re-election bid. the purpose of that call was to tie Congressionally appropriated funds to Ukraine to Zelensky's cooperation in finding dirt on Hunter Biden that Trump could use against Joe Biden. Trump was impeached for this self-professed "perfect" call. Bribery is a crime that involves persuading someone to act in one's favor, typically illegally or dishonestly, by a gift of money or other inducement.

To be sure, the charges Biden faces are serious; but to equate the actions of a private citizen to the actions of the President of the United States bound by oath and the Constitution is not only illogically a false equivalence, but downright folly. Biden is not the first private citizen to face these types of charges. Trump is the first president to engage in the conduct that compels investigation into the most serious charges ever faced by a sitting president.

Those Republicans who boast some level of comfort out of making such a comparison. or believe this provides cover for Trump by deflecting from the seriousness of the charges he faces, are only fooling themselves and their supporters.

Dr. Spock of Star Trek fame would have a field day with the illogic demonstrated by these Republicans. And by analogy from this great historic TV show, Trump has gone where no president has gone before.

The bottom line here is that no person is above the law. Not private citizen Biden. Not former President Trump. Engaging in illogical, fallacious thinking may provide a false sense of comfort or security, but it will not help the latter.

THIS IS IN THE "BE CAREFUL WHAT YOU WISH FOR" CATEGORY

Considering the current polls, Republicans are gleeful, chortling at their prospects in November for taking over both houses of Congress.

Should this happen, they promise to investigate:

> all members of the House committee looking into January 6's riot at the capital;
>
> those Republicans who testified against Donald Trump at the committee hearings;
>
> and just about everyone of influence who at any time dared to question Trump and his ardent loyalists.

They also promise to impeach President Biden. For what? Oh, they'll think of something. All they need is a majority in the House of Representatives to decide what "high crimes and misdemeanors" means—and in their topsy-turvy alternative world, it can mean whatever they want it to mean. Remember, this is the party of alternative facts. (The Republicans will never get the required 2/3 majority of the Senate to convict anyway, but this won't bother House Republicans hellbent on revenge.)

Certainly, the economy is the primary motivating factor in elections; people generally vote their pocketbooks. Voters also generally want things to be better than what the incumbent party offers. But in equating their pocketbook with wanting things to be better, there is a tendency to overlook other, potentially more profound, matters.

Assuming the economy is the primary reason for voting, the logical next question is what do the Republicans offer than is better than what the Democrats offer.

Historically, we know the Republicans' laissez-faire policies gave us the Great Depression; they also steadfastly favored isolationism and promoted appeasing Hitler, which allowed Germany to build its military might. (Pearl Harbor put a stop to their obstructionism and appeasement.)

Similarly from history, we know the Democrats took us out of the Great Depression in part by creating Social Security and other programs to jumpstart the economy, ae well as those that provided controls on the previous free-wheeling banking and securities systems favored by Republicans.

We also know from history how the Democrats mobilized the economy and built our military might that ultimately led us to victory in World War II. The Democrats also gave us civil rights and social justice legislation that Republicans vigorously opposed.

To this day, Republicans oppose similar types of legislation on the grounds that it impedes states' rights and costs too much money. The Republicans still give tax breaks for the wealthy and favorable treatment for big corporations; their last major fait accompli was in 2017. Perhaps if they required these beneficiaries to pay their fair share, there would be enough revenue to support the programs they oppose, but that's another matter.

We know that while they rail at Biden for high prices and rampant inflation, they vigorously oppose passing legislation that would address these problems, most likely because they simply can't—or won't—give Biden and the Democrats anything they can use against the Republicans in the leadup to the November election cycle.

Here's what else the Republicans offer. They offer fear; fear of "socialism," "radical leftist indoctrination" etc.--anything that arouses anger and resentment against the Democrats that their supporters swallow whole. What they won't talk about is what they offered America in just the past 18 months: an attack on Democracy driven by corruption in the White House and in the halls of Congress; calling those who testified truthfully under oath traitors; branding as patriots those who attacked the capital, injuring law enforcement officers and others, and damaging sanctified property. Republicans also offer defiance of subpoenas and pleas for pardons.

If, as Shakespeare said, the past is prologue, then we can expect more legislative benefits for the wealthy, including more corporate welfare. We can expect programs for the vast majority of Americans in the middle class and those less fortunate to be scuttled. We can expect more corruption in the White House and in Congress. We can certainly expect what they've promised: vengeful attacks on those who stood up for the truth and didn't cower in the face of threats. And we can expect to see more begging for pardons leading up to the 2024 presidential election. (We certainly won't see Republicans defying congressional subpoenas because they won't be investigating Republican shenanigans.)

Republicans need to stop telling us what they're against and start telling us what they're going to do, not for revenge or payback, and not for the wealthy or Big Business, but for the middle class and those less fortunate--those whose numbers are far greater than the upper tier that gets these targeted benefits.

Don't tell us how great Republicans are for banning books, telling school officials what they can and can't teach, promoting discrimination against people's personal lifestyles you don't like, etc. Tell us what specific programs and policies you are going to implement for the benefit of the many, not the very few. Remember then-President Trump promised to repeal and replace Obamacare with a great Republican health care plan. We are still waiting for that program to be revealed. (It never existed, and doesn't exist today.)

And stop handing out the usual platitudes and buzzwords such as limited government, less taxes, real conservative values, law and order and personal responsibility.

If Republicans really believed in limited government, they wouldn't be telling schools, colleges and universities what they can and, more importantly, can't teach, and telling Americans what they can and can't read or say.

If they really believed is less taxes, they wouldn't have made the 2017 tax cuts for the wealthy permanent, while sunsetting tax cuts for the middle class in 2025.

If they truly believed in law and order, they would have roundly condemned the January 6 riot that led to the death of several law enforcement officers and injuries to dozens more. They would have praised those who testified under oath and condemned those who snubbed their noses at subpoenas and who sought presidential pardons.

If they really believed in personal responsibility, they wouldn't have called those who attacked the capital patriots.

They would have supported investigating criminal activity associated with that attack. They would have aggressively criticized those who tried to avoid accountability by not honoring subpoenas or by seeking pardons.

And please identify those "real conservatives" and what is meant by "conservative values." Are the "real conservatives" those who attacked the capital, fomented violence, rejected subpoenas and sought pardons? Or are the "real conservatives" those who testified under oath and continue to offer evidence of criminal conduct in the White House and Congress? Tell us how to separate the "real conservatives" from the fake ones.

Are "conservative values" represented by the instigating of violence based on a known lie that led to the attack on the capital? Are these "values" represented by standing idly by as the violence continued? Are "conservative values" demonstrated by those who rejected subpoenas and sought pardons? Or by supporting Christian nationalism, or advocating that the Christian religion direct the government? Pray tell, please tell us.

It's really very simple: tell us specifically what you're going to do to benefit most Americans, how you're going to do it, and how this will help our nation.

It is doubtful Republicans will answer these questions. They will probably add to their enemies list those who dare to ask them.

So far, all the Republican promise is revenge and payback. But what about those policies and programs to factually make America great? So far, silence.

The past is prologue. When voters go to the polls in November, remember events over the past two years. And recall this poignant warning: Be careful what you wish for.

THE THREAT THAT WILL END DEMOCRACY IN AMERICA

Awhile back, I wrote an article on how the Constitution could be amended, even re-written. At that time, I wasn't fully aware of the conservatives' game plan, both long- and short-term. I was primarily engaging in an academic exercise of constitutional "what ifs."

I didn't know or expect then that what I wrote would precisely match what is the conservatives' plan for the nation's future.

Based on a series of articles setting out the conservatives' long-range plans, the prospects for a complete re-write of the nation's charter that has guided us since 1788 ominously appears just over the horizon.

In my article, I noted that there are two ways to change the Constitution: The first is for a two-thirds majority of Congress to propose an amendment, with three-fourths of states ratifying it. All 27 of the current amendments to the Constitution were added through this process. The last time an amendment was adopted this way was in 1992. Considering the partisanship that divides Congress, using this approach to amend the Constitution appears untenable for the foreseeable future.

The second method — never before tried or accomplished — calls for two-thirds of several states to call a convention. This power is vested solely with state legislatures, who could "pass and ratify amendments without a governor's signature, Congress' intervention, or any input from the president."

A convention called by state legislatures could re-write the nation's Constitution in its entirety.

It would take 34 states to call a convention. It would take 38 states to ratify the convention's final product. Currently, 30 state legislatures are controlled by the Republican Party. All that is necessary is for four more to join in for a convention to be called. Add four more states onto that, and what is written becomes our new Constitution.

What could a state-legislature-called Constitutional Convention do in re-writing the Constitution? Use your imagination. Think of what Republicans have promised regarding constitutional rights, civil rights, social legislation, church-dominating government, book banning, academic freedom trumped, free speech and free press curtailed, relaxation of libel laws, revamping education curriculum, the unitary or authoritarian presidency, a remodeled judiciary, and on and on and on.

The entirety of the conservative agenda would be written into the nation's organic charter. The Bill of Rights could become unrecognizable. For a snapshot of what life could be like, read up on what economic life in America was like in the 1930s as our nation struggled to survive the 1929 stock market crash. Learn what life was like for the "others" in the 1950s and early 1960s.

Admittedly, under the current political environment, the prospects of such a constitutional convention scenario are somewhat slim. But as this article makes abundantly clear, this plan is part of the conservatives' long-term strategy.

Note the names of current political figures in the article below who support this approach, such as Donald Trump and Ron DeSantis. While Trump is aging, DeSantis is in his early 40s and plans to be around a long time. And there are many other young conservatives in Congress, state legislatures and local governments who aspire to greater heights and hope to be around a long time, exerting their influence on our federal, as well as state and local governments.

"THE WHEELS OF JUSTICE TURN SLOWLY, BUT GRIND EXCEEDINGLY FINE"

As a lawyer, I heard this phrase quite often. It means that even though justice may not be done quickly when it finally happens the criminal will not escape from receiving his or her full punishment.

On September 11, 2001, we suffered the worst attack by a foreign entity on American soil when hijacked planes crashed into the Twin Towers in New York and the Pentagon in Washington. A third plane headed for either the Capitol where Congress was in session, or the White House, was commandeered by the courageous passengers and forced it to crash in an open field in Pennsylvania. This attack on America was planned and carried out by al-Qaida.

On January 6, 2021, we suffered the worst attack on American soil by domestic entities when, stoked by a lie of a rigged election by President Donald Trump, a large group of right-wing supporters attacked our nation's capital, leading to several deaths, injuries to more than 140 law enforcement officers and significant damage to the Capitol itself. The purpose of this attack was to keep Donald Trump in power after having lost every one of his post-election lawsuits in the various courts of our nation and states, including the Supreme Court. He was aided and abetted by several members of Congress and White House staffers.

Within a 24-hour period, two events took place that proves what is quoted above.

First, a U.S. drone strike killed al-Qaida leader Ayman al-Zawahri in a CIA operation carried out in Kabul, Afghanistan. He played key roles in the 9/11 attacks and bombings of U.S. embassies, and became leader of the terrorist group after Osama bin Laden was killed in 2011.

Second, a day later, Guy Reffitt, an ardent Donald Trump supporter from Texas who tried to storm the Capitol while armed with a gun, helmet and body armor, and threatened House Speaker Nancy Pelosi, was sentenced to more than seven years in prison. He was the first January 6 defendant to go to trial. Others who participated in the attack have been sentenced and are serving their time; others are slated to go on trial. Perhaps some will reconsider and take plea deals.

Recently, one of Trump's ardent loyalists, Steve Bannon, was convicted of contempt of Congress for refusing to honor a subpoena to testify under oath about events pertaining to January 6.

Others who defied congressional subpoenas, most notably Trump's Chief of Staff Mark Meadows and advisor Peter Navarro, have been similarly charged and are awaiting trial.

So far, none of the government actors whose names are connected to the planning and execution of the January 6 attack have testified under oath.

And then we come to Donald Trump. The testimony of Republicans, including those who worked in the Trump White House, have offered damning evidence against him to the House investigating committee of potential crimes of sedition, conspiracy to commit sedition, obstruction of justice, dereliction of duty, witness tampering, etc.

Evidence also implicates several members of Congress and White House staff, including legal counsel.

The question arises, will Donald Trump face criminal charges? The prospect of a former president of the United States criminally charged or indicted for multiple felonies that could put him behind bars for the rest of his life is a daunting thought. Only a pardon by President Gerald Ford prevented Richard Nixon from suffering that fate.

But a presidential pardon is out of the question, at least until 2025.

A second question is whether any members of Congress or Trump staffers will also face a battery of criminal charges.

Attorney General Merrick Garland said just the other day, "no one is above the law."

Justice may not be done quickly, but when it is, the criminal will not escape from receiving full punishment. This applies to everyone, including those who hold high office.

SEN. LINDSEY GRAHAM IS GRASPING AT STRAWS

As he said he would, Lindsey Graham is challenging a subpoena issued in Georgia in connection with that state's investigation into contact he made with the Georgia secretary of state regarding the state's 2020 presidential election results.

In his efforts to avoid testifying under oath, Graham, through his lawyers, cites a provision of the Constitution that they say "provides absolute protection against inquiry into Senator Graham's legislative acts." They also argue "sovereign immunity" prevents a local prosecutor from summoning a senator "to face a state ad hoc investigatory body."

It seems he's using the same type of lawyers who Donald Trump used in losing every case he brought challenging that election.

First, a "legislative act" means an "act passed by a legislative body." A court can't compel inquiry into reasons why a legislator voted a certain way. This is known as mental process inquiry, and as a practicing lawyer for many years in Florida government, I used this defense successfully many times. Calling the Georgia secretary of state to inquire about an election result affecting his party's president is not a "legislative act." Asking a legislator to testify under oath on potential criminal conduct of another is not a "legislative act."

Second, "sovereign immunity" is "a legal doctrine whereby a sovereign or state can't commit a legal wrong and is immune from civil suit or criminal prosecution." I used this defense successfully on numerous occasions as well. It means just that: immunity from civil suit or criminal prosecution. Graham is not being sued, and is not facing criminal prosecution. He is simply being subpoenaed to testify under oath.

That's two strikes.

This absolute immunity defense is neither a new nor recent claim. In the case of Trump v. Vance, the Manhattan district attorney's office, acting on behalf of a grand jury, issued to subpoena on Trump's personal accounting firm for his personal and business financial records. In the Supreme Court, Trump's personal lawyer and the U.S. Justice Department made two arguments: the president has "absolute immunity" from the criminal process; and prosecutors must meet a "heightened need" standard for issuing a subpoena to a sitting president.

The 7-2 majority, in an opinion by Chief Justice John Roberts Jr., rejected both arguments. In reaching that decision, Roberts first turned to a maxim that dates to a 1742 English parliamentary debate: "the public has a right to every man's evidence."

That is true of our justice system, he said, and since the earliest days of the Republic, he added, "every man" has included the president.

The" every man's evidence" line is repeated from an earlier case rejecting Richard Nixon's similar defense during the Watergate investigation.

If a president can be compelled to testify under oath, certainly a United States senator can on matters that don't include why he voted on legislation.

That's strike three.

WHEN BELIEF AND OPINION BECOME FACT

The headline says: **More than 100 GOP primary winners back Trump's false fraud claims.**

There are two possibilities in play here. These folks either know the facts but fear the wrath of Donald Trump and Trumpism, or they truly believe Trump's false fraud claims to be true.

There is danger in either possibility. First, believing as true what you know is false solely because you fear your leader can easily result in acting in a way that you know to be wrong—or perhaps criminal—solely to please the authoritarian. This is not how a democracy functions; it is precisely the way a dictator or despot survives.

Second, if they really believe Trump's lies, then the propaganda that is the Big Lie has succeeded in indoctrinating and brainwashing these people. As Stella Payton said: "Whatever you believe to be true, whether it is true or not; if you believe it, then to you it becomes the truth." To these candidates, as well as many officeholders and others, facts don't matter. It's their belief and opinion that constitute their facts.

Recall this statement attributed to Nazi Propaganda Minister Joseph Goebbels: "If you tell a lie big enough and keep repeating it, people will eventually come to believe it. The lie can be maintained only for such time as the State can shield the people from the political, economic and/or military consequences of the lie. It thus becomes vitally important for the State to use all of its powers to repress dissent, for the truth is the mortal enemy of the lie, and thus by extension, the truth is the greatest enemy of the State."

The swapping fact for belief is known as the illusory truth effect. The inherent danger here is the tendency to believe false information to be correct after repeated exposure. Re-read Goebbels' statement and compare it to the headline above.

In a 2015 study, researchers discovered that familiarity can overpower reason, and that continuing to refute that a certain statement is wrong can affect the hearer's beliefs. Researchers attributed the illusory truth effect's impact on participants who knew the correct answer to begin with, but were persuaded to believe otherwise through the repetition of a falsehood. This illusory truth effect plays a significant role in such fields as election campaigns, advertising, news media, and political propaganda.

It is impossible to engage in a meaningful dialogue and reason with those who steadfastly rely on a known lie as being true. The fact that more than 60 lawsuits making this false claim were rejected by every court that considered it means nothing to those who treat their beliefs and opinions are fact.

The further danger behind this attitude that belief and opinion are fact should be self-evident. The purpose of reliance on facts is that it provides an agreed-upon common ground. If people can remain fixated in the self-righteousness of their beliefs or opinions, and refuse to be "confused by facts," then reality becomes a matter of belief rather than what can be objectively proven. We then become a nation of men where there is no general consensus.

To be sure, there are occasions when it is perfectly legitimate to form a belief and express an opinion based on available information. For example, if you're standing outside and see dark clouds forming, and feel drops of water on your head, you may certainly believe that it's about to rain. Only after there is a deluge, or the dark clouds dissipate with no bad weather, can you conclude whether your initial opinion or belief was correct. Another example is if you have pain in your mouth, you can conclude that you have a toothache. A trip to the dentist will either confirm this, or find a different cause. In both instances, you relied on your best information at the time.

There is a vast difference between fact and opinion or belief; yet, alarmingly, research shows that most people believe their opinions are facts. We incorrectly believe that our thoughts are correct. In short, the attitude is if we think it, it must be true.

The truth is that a fact is a statement that can be supported to be true or false by objective data or evidence. In contrast, an opinion is a personal expression of a person's feelings or thoughts that may or may not be based in data. Indeed, many of our opinions are based on emotions, personal history, and values—all of which can be completely unsupported by meaningful evidence. A belief is a state or habit of mind in which trust or confidence is placed in some person or thing; something that is accepted, considered to be true, or held as an opinion.

No one would want or expect a journalist to give offer opinions as fact, without any supporting evidence. No one would want a lawyer to offer his/her beliefs and opinions to a court with no supporting facts. No one would want a judge to issue rulings based solely on his beliefs without any facts.

This truism is certainly applicable here: You are entitled to your opinions; you are not entitled to your own facts.

Fact-driven professions such as education, journalism, law and science could not survive in a belief- or opinion-driven world. Indeed, there isn't a profession, occupation or vocation that could survive if only beliefs and opinions mattered, with no facts or other empirical evidence. The dangerous and draconian effects this would have on the consuming public should be obvious.

Studies show that opinions without facts most commonly lead to a series of bad decisions. Opinions are your truth. Your truth can be wrong to others, but not to yourself. (Hopefully, you see the bad logic here.)

The emotion of opinions can hurt others. It hurts when someone says, "You're not doing well in this job." The reason it hurts is because it is someone else's opinion of you. Opinions are like painful judgments.

Opinions blind logic. Opinions can be very illogical. In a way, opinions are blind to logic. A person with a strong opinion cannot always see the full truth. Yet, this person will feel very strongly, and be convicted by his opinion.

Communication stops when we rely solely on the emotional aspect of opinion. If you want to stop positive communication, then speak only in emotion and opinion, and leave out the facts. The conversation will be one sided, and you will always be right. However, the conversation will not be productive or beneficial.

The search for facts and other forms of credible evidence that constitute the truth must never give way to belief and opinion alone as fact. Democracy can't survive without facts as a common denominator.

80-YEAR-OLD MAN PROVES AN ASSAULT RIFLE ISN'T NEEDED FOR SELF-DEFENSE

This is a feel-good story that could have had a tragic ending. An old man defended himself and his property by shooting a criminal bearing an assault rifle.

No doubt this demonstrates the importance of having a firearm for self-defense.

No one would disagree with that.

But notice what else is important in this story. Only the thugs had assault rifles. The weapon used for self-defense was a shotgun, not an assault rifle.

This article says the guns were stolen, as was the car they were driving.

The store owner proves no one needs an assault rifle for self-defense. The four thugs prove how easy it is to get access to these weapons. In this case, just break into a store that sells them to the general public.

Presumably, they could have walked into a gun shop and said to the clerk "Excuse me, I'd like to buy an assault rifle."

The clerk could have said "Sure, would you like me to gift-wrap it for you."

I don't mean to make light of a deadly serious subject. I do mean to make a point.

Of course, four thugs hellbent on committing crimes would have found other weapons, but considering how these assault rifles have been used to commit mass murder in public places, brandishing one certainly raises the fear level of law-abiding citizens. Fortunately, this store owner wasn't paralyzed by fear; he reacted appropriately. He did suffer a heart attack, but is expected to make a full recovery.

Still, it's well-nigh impossible to get one's hands on these weapons of mass murder if they're not available for sale or possession to the general public.

Ban them.

WHO ARE THE GREAT CONSERVATIVE THINKERS?

Conservatives continue to lambast Democrats, calling them socialists, radicals, etc. But when they called them dumb and uneducated, I wondered who those great thinkers are who are guiding the conservative viewpoint, and are smarter and better educated than these Democrats. In other words, who are the great conservative thinkers who have this superior intelligence and who never do dumb things?

Is it Donald Trump? He couldn't admit he lost his re-election bid, told a lie about it, instigated violence, continues to tell that lie, and sits comfortably in Mar-A-Lago while many of his supporters languish in jail or await their date with the criminal justice system. While president, he also said there some nice Neo-Nazis, and that people could have ingested disinfectant like bleach to cure COVID.

Perhaps it's Sen. Josh Hawley, who cheered on the January 6 rioters, only to be seen running from them shortly thereafter. He also accused men of appearing stuck in a cycle of "idleness and pornography and video games."

How about Sen. Ted Cruz, who flew to Cancun while his constituents froze during a winter storm that hit Texas, and who bragged about a painting of himself while arguing before the Supreme Court

Maybe it's Rep. Lauren Boebert who thinks the separation between church and state is nonsense, and that the Christian religion (or her version of it) should be directing the government.

Rep. Marjorie Taylor Greene? In 2018, a poorly maintained electrical grid sparked a California wildfire that killed 84 people. In a Facebook post, she falsely suggested that a bank controlled by Rothschild family members, who are Jewish; a utility company responsible for the fire, and then-Gov. Jerry Brown, all had a compelling motive to spark the blaze: clearing the path for a high-speed rail project Brown wanted. She also floated the possibility that the fires could have been started by "lasers or blue beams of light" shot down from space by allies of Brown who were said to be in the solar energy industry. In November 2018, Greene shot a video in which she talked about the 9/11 terrorist attacks, referring to a "so-called" plane that crashed into the Pentagon. She added, "It's odd, there's never any evidence shown for a plane in the Pentagon."

How about Rep. Jim Jordan, who is slated to become chairman of the House Judiciary Committee if the Republicans take over the House in November. After repeatedly arguing that Trump's election bid was stolen, said after receiving the Presidential Medal of Freedom from him that he never said the election was stolen. He is one of several members of Congress currently under investigation for his involvement in the attack on the capital.

Maybe Rep. Paul Gosar, who photoshopped anime video he posted on Twitter in which he is shown killing New York Democratic Rep. Alexandria Ocasio-Cortez and threatening President Joe Biden.

How about Rep. Matt Gaetz, who is currently under investigation for possibly having sex with a 17-year-old and then paying for her to travel over state lines, and was one of 20 Republicans who voted "No" to reauthorize an anti-human trafficking law.

What about Gov. Ron DeSantis? He created a new police security office to investigate allegations of voter fraud despite admitting that state elections ran smoothly, and there never was, or is, evidence of widespread voter fraud in Florida. He supports curriculum cleansing, book banning, and making it more difficult — and increasing the potential jail times — for state residents who peacefully protest and demonstrate, actions protected by the First Amendment.

Gov. Greg Abbott? He supports eliminating the right to an abortion because this "will get rid of rapists."

Perhaps it's Alex Jones, head of Infowars whose repeated lies—among numerous others--that the Sandy Hook Elementary School mass shooting was a hoax has finally caught up with him. He has filed for bankruptcy to avoid the damages he has to pay for his hurtful lies. When, on the witness stand, he was confronted with evidence that he lied under oath, he finally caved, saying Sandy Hook was real. Because of his comeuppance and day of reckoning, he faces total destruction of his career by his own hand.

Then there's Fox host and entertainer Tucker Carlson, who after being sued for libel by Dominion Voting Systems for claiming without a shred of evidence that the company rigged the election machines to register Trump votes for Biden, is being defended by Fox News as being an entertainer whose statements are not to be believed.

Maybe it's the lawyers, like Rudy Giuliani, Sidney Powell, and those who willingly and knowingly followed them into public embarrassment for having lost every lawsuit they filed supporting Trump's Big Lie. These lawyers were schooled in the necessity for having facts to back up their legal arguments—something they obviously overlooked.

Perhaps it's John Eastman and those legal eagles who offered a theory unfounded in American constitutional law that a sitting vice president can reject electoral college votes based on his belief alone. Eastman is under investigation for his uniformly rejected theory.

Maybe these great minds are among those members of Congress who back Trump's lie and still believe the election was stolen from him. It could be those who defied congressional subpoenas in connection with the January 6 investigation, or sought pardons from Trump.

Maybe they're among those Trump-backed election denier candidates who won in key primary races.

Perhaps prominent conservative thinkers are among those who voted for, or get their information from, these people.

The examples noted above are certainly not comprehensive; they are just a few of the things these people said or did that might be considered by conservatives as representative of outstanding intelligence, wisdom and judgment demonstrative of highly educated people—and demonstrate to the world how dumb and uneducated Democrats are.

I remember those who were great conservative thinkers of the past. William F. Buckley, Jr. Barry Goldwater. Ronald Reagan. John McCain. What would they say in reaction to those whose names appear above? Would they consider those above to be great conservative thinkers?

When the conservatives castigate Democrats, it would behoove them to identify those who they believe reside(s) at the fount of today's conservative thought.

TURNING A DEMOCRACY INTO AN AUTOCRACY

Relying on his "ours is a government of laws, not of men," and his law-and-order theme, Florida Gov. Ron DeSantis suspended the Hillsborough County state attorney for refusing to enforce laws on abortion and transgender surgery.

He did this before the state Supreme Court decides cases based on the privacy right specifically set out in the state constitution and is independent of the US Supreme Court's ruling on abortion. Remember, these are purely private decisions that don't harm others.

When he says "our nation is a government of laws, not of men," what he really means is a government of laws made by his men (and women) and enforced according to the will of his men (and women). His "men" made these laws against the will of the majority of Americans, and they will be enforced regardless, even before the state judiciary chimes in, or he will remove from office anyone who dares to question him, fails to do his bidding, or fails to move in lockstep with him and his "men."

His "men" get to define what law and order means, generally following a certain religious mantra, and woe to those who dare to stand up and disagree.

By the way, his "government of laws" claim rings hollow. As the federal government aims at expanding protections for LGBTQ people, DeSantis and his state agencies are vowing to dodge those safeguards. In a memo from the Florida education department, state schools were told to ignore nondiscrimination guidance from the U.S. Department of Education and Department of Agriculture.

So, it's perfectly ok for him to ignore federal law he doesn't like, but it's not ok for a state attorney to refuse to prosecute under a law DeSantis likes. That's hypocrisy. He needs to be reminded about the Constitution's supremacy clause that makes federal law supreme to state law.

This is a classic example of turning a democracy into an autocracy.

THE REPUBLICAN PARTY'S GOAL: A STRANGLEHOLD ON FEDERAL AND STATE GOVERNMENTS

From statements made over the past few years by Republican Party leaders, the party's goal is without question to achieve a stranglehold on all three branches of the federal government, and as many state governments as possible.

The party has short-term as well as long-term plans to achieve that goal.

The party's most immediate plan is to gain control of Congress. Polls indicate the party will regain a majority in the House after the November midterm elections. The senate is in the iffy column right now.

Control of one chamber means the Republicans can investigate anyone for anything to their heart's content. If it's the House, they can impeach Biden for whatever they decide is "high crimes and misdemeanors." Control of both means they can pass any and all legislation they want. There is only one wrinkle in the latter: President Biden's veto pen.

To turn legislation into law, however, they will need to elect an accommodating president. Their plan after the mid-terms is to do just that in 2024.

These two are their two short-term plans.

Once they have the executive and legislative branches under control, they will move ahead simultaneously with three plans that may take more time.

First, they will attempt to purge moderates from the party. This is a faction that has become increasingly small since the 1990s anyway.

Currently, there are about 50 House members and two to four senators (Sens. Collins and Murkowski, and perhaps Romney and Sasse) who might be considered moderate. You can bet that the hardcore conservative wing that has been growing over the past few years will either force these moderates to cave in and conform, or do whatever it takes to relegate them to the back bench and make them useless outcasts, or drive them out of Congress by resignation or defeat at the polls.

Second, they will attempt to take over the judiciary. It is a plan that may take a few years beyond 2025.

The number of federal judges, both trial and appellate, changes quite often. Currently, there are about 407 federal judges appointed by Democrats; 486 by Republicans. Donald Trump appointed 229 judges during his four years; Joe Biden has appointed 69 during his first 18 months in office. This averages out to roughly three to five a month. If the senate turns Republican, Biden's appointments will languish until they get a Republican in the White House in 2025 (so the party's plan goes.)

No doubt Biden will try to get as many judges appointed and confirmed between now and the end of this year.

Assuming he gets several more confirmed, and some Republican-appointed judges either take senior status or leave the judiciary, the number of Democrat-appointed judges will go up over the next few months, while the number of Republican appointees will drop, leaving a relatively even balance in party appointees.

These numbers, however, will change dramatically should a Republican take the White House in 2025.

Why is the judiciary so important? You will recall that Trump's re-election litigation was rejected by many of his own appointees, including his Supreme Court appointees.

The party hopes that by getting a larger federal judiciary of like-minded conservatives, there will be far more conservative victories than defeats in the courts. Indeed, they hope to eliminate any prospects of the latter.

If a Republican is elected president, and has a solid senate behind him, he/she will presumably appoint over 200 judges in the first term; over two terms, the president could well appoint over 400 judges, virtually recasting the entire federal judiciary. If Republicans elect back-to-back presidents, the effect on the judiciary should be self-evident.

This is precisely why the judiciary is so important.

Their third plan will take substantially longer: supermajority control of Congress to effectively re-write the Constitution. It takes a 2/3 vote of each house to propose an amendment to the federal Constitution. That's 290 members for the house and 67 for the senate. This supermajority vote allows Congress to propose any amendment it wishes. All that remains if for two-thirds of the state legislatures to ratify to become law; that's 38 states. Currently, 30 state legislatures are in Republican hands. The party needs eight more states to accomplish amending the Constitution in this manner. (The second method, by constitutional convention, requires 34 state legislatures to call for a convention, with 38 state legislatures required for ratification. Republicans are only four states away from the first step under this method.)

The party will work exceedingly hard over the next several years to try to reach these numbers.

Considering the current level of partisanship, the second method is far more difficult than the first. However, the Republicans will do whatever is necessary to eliminate the current level of partisanship and elect their like-minded to office. And they will work the states needed to call a constitutional convention.

And then there's that presidential veto power. It takes a 2/3 vote in both the house and senate to overrule a presidential veto. This means that even if a Democrat is elected president, a Republican supermajority in the Congress can render the veto power a nullity.

Here are the visions of sugar plums dancing in the Republican Party leaders' heads:

A right-wing president in the White House, along with his like-minded loyalists in key executive positions; a Congress made up strongly of like-minded officials; and a judiciary comprised of like-minded lawyers.

This is their jackpot.

Welcome to our brave new world!

HOW DO THE REPUBLICANS PLAN TO GOVERN?

The other day, I wrote about the Republican Party's goal of a complete and substantial takeover of the federal government. This will be accomplished, according to the plan, once the House and Senate are comfortably in the party's hands, the party regains the White House in 2024, and dozens—indeed hundreds-- of federal judges are appointed and confirmed.

Currently, the party is co-opted by the far-right wing. Assuming they retain the upper hand, what can our nation expect? How do the Republicans plan to govern?

Let's look at some evidence.

During Donald Trump's years in the White House, he repeatedly cozied up to Russia's Vladimir Putin. Many Republicans wondered why he would do such a thing. Why, they asked, would Trump become buddies with a socialist or a communist? The answer is because Putin is neither a communist nor a socialist, and neither is Russia.

That Putin is a socialist or communist is a matter of perception; it is not reality. For example, in a recent poll, 52 percent of Republicans agreed that Russia was operating under Communism, despite the country not being Communist since the Soviet Union dissolved in 1991. Among all Americans, 42 percent thought that Russia was Communist, including 44 percent of Democrats.

Another 18 percent of Republicans, as well as 15 percent of Trump voters, claimed that Russia was operating under a "Socialist" system, something that is also not true.

On paper, Russia is a federal democratic state. In practice, however, many regard it as a dictatorship built around one man, Putin.

Trump genuflected to Putin for one reason: Trump likes strong leaders. Putin is a strong leader. In fact, Putin is an authoritarian who practices enforcing strict obedience to authority, especially that of the government—his government--at the expense of personal freedom.

Trump fancies himself as strong leader; many of his words and actions fit the definition of a classic authoritarian.

Next up is Hungarian Prime Minister Viktor Orban. On paper, Hungary is a multiparty parliamentary democracy. The unicameral National Assembly (parliament) exercises legislative authority. It elects the president (the head of state) every five years.

In practice, Orban is an authoritarian who has extolled the value of racial purity, is vehemently anti-immigration and has cultivated close ties with Russia's Putin. He is widely criticized around the world for systematically dismantling his country's nascent democracy during his 12 years in power — but that hasn't stopped him from emerging as a darling of many on the right in America.

Orbán recently addressed the Conservative Political Action Conference, known as CPAC, in Dallas. He told a cheering crowd of conference delegates that he and other conservatives were in a battle to protect Western civilization against the forces of liberalism and mass migration. He said previously that Hungarians "do not want to become peoples of mixed race." One former adviser, who has since resigned, referred to those comments as "a pure Nazi speech worthy of Goebbels." Orbán, who came to power in 2010, has increasingly clamped down on political opposition and press freedom, consolidating his power further over the last two elections.

Putin, Orban and Trump. And the mini-Trumps.

Trump has latched on to the authoritarian mold, and the millions who follow him and his loyalists believe he can do no wrong and support authoritarianism.

The facts are uncontroverted that he lied about his election loss, knew he lied, yet convinced his followers to commit serious crimes on his behalf for the sole purpose of remaining in power illegally. January 6 is clear evidence of that—evidence of his culpability offered under oath by members of his own party. "Rigged election" repeated often enough becomes the truth. The message here is clear. Once the lie is accepted, it becomes truth or reality. Facts don't matter.

A significant part of the authoritarian plan is the use of repeated lies, harking to Nazi Propaganda Minister Joseph Goebbels' "a lie repeated often enough becomes the truth."

Repeat the Republican buzzwords often enough, and they become the truth. This how indoctrination occurs; this is how authoritarians brainwash their people.

Despite this, Trump is worshipped because his loyalists believe his pity-party line that he's the most persecuted president in history. They refuse to believe the evidence of his criminal conduct that is the cause of his self-inflicted woes. They believe that it's all noise, a partisan hit job, even though the witnesses against him are Republicans, including those who worked for him in the White House.

When loyalists tried to pass off the capital attack on Antifa, that was quickly and laughingly debunked. Then the Republican National Committee said it was just some zealous Trump supporters engaging in "legitimate public discourse."

Facts simply don't matter to his worshippers. They readily accept his lies, and the RNC lie, as fact and truth.

Some true believers say the Christian church should control government, that social security should be taxed (Sen. Rick Scott) or, along with Medicare, renewed periodically (Sen. Ron Johnson) even as they claim to be for less taxes and in favor of these vital programs. Some example of less taxes; some example of support.

A key form of authoritarianism is Fascism. Fascism is a far-right, authoritarian, ultranationalist political ideology, philosophy and movement, characterized by a dictatorial leader, centralized autocracy, militarism, forcible suppression of opposition, belief in a natural social hierarchy, subordination of individual interests for the good of the nation and race, and strong regimentation of society and the economy.

Compare the statements of Putin and Orban with the definition above. The connection is obvious.

When conservatives rail against the evils of socialism and communism, ask them if they oppose the evils of fascism. Chances are you'll be greeted by silence, then a deer-in-the-headlight look, followed by further rants about the Democrats. Apparently, they hate socialism and communism, but give a pass to fascism.

Here is yet another form of propaganda designed to indoctrinate: repeated use of the word freedom.

Not to be outdone by Trump, and following the Putin/Orban method, Florida Gov. Ron DeSantis proudly boasts that Florida is the freest state in America.

He says banning books he and his minions don't like is freedom. Removing subjects from school curriculum is freedom.

Freedom of speech and press apply only to those who agree with him; those who disagree face punishment.

Without any evidence of fraud in any election results bearing on the 2020 presidential election, several states, including Florida, changed their voting laws in the name of protecting against nonexistent fraud. Those changes are designed to accomplish one thing: to assure that Republicans are elected to office regardless of the vote totals. Tossing out the fraud nonsense, this is the only remaining reason that makes sense—except to those who claim to know better because, well, they just know better.

So, what can we expect from a Republican-dominated government? More of the same: repression and control defined as freedom. Review the statements of Putin, and those of Orban that the audience cheered applauded. This is the authoritarian's way. This is what fascism looks like.

TRUMP AND BIDEN LEGISLATIVE COMPARISON—THERE IS NONE.

Donald Trump loves to call Joe Biden "Sleepy Joe." His cronies and loyalists gleefully chortle at Biden's weakness, fatigue, missteps, etc., etc., etc. They love to compare him with their "stable genius," the man who considers himself such a great president that he says he should be on Mount Rushmore, and even considered giving himself the Congressional Medal of Honor.

Ok, so let's compare actual major legislative accomplishments between the two.

Trump had four years; we'll consider Biden's over 18 months.

The signature piece of legislation during Trump's years was The Tax Cuts and Jobs Act in 2017. This provided for permanent tax cuts for the wealthy and middle-class tax cuts that expire in 2025. It passed through the reconciliation process, thereby avoiding the filibuster.

At the time it passed, the Congressional Budget Office estimated the measure would add about $2 trillion to the national debt over ten years. The Tax and Jobs Act did not increase employment or wages as the Republicans expected; those actually dipped slightly as corporations used the tax cuts primarily to buy back their stock, making it more valuable.

Trump also touts his three Supreme Court appointees. The now-majority conservative Court overruled a constitutional right for the first time in American history, and has set its sights on overruling additional constitutional, civil and social rights of Americans.

That's if for Donald Trump.

Now, here's the Biden major legislative accomplishments so far.

For 2022:

1. The Inflation Reduction Act of 2022. (This bill passed the Senate and is expected to pass the House this week.)

It will invest about $300 billion toward reducing the deficit.

The bill's purpose is to lower the cost of certain prescription drugs by enabling the government to negotiate the prices of expensive drugs for Medicare, a policy most nations already have. It also caps the cost of insulin at $35 a month for people on Medicare (Republicans stripped out of the bill a similar protection for those on private insurance). It makes corporations making $1 billion or more in income pay a 15% minimum tax, and it will tax stock buybacks at 1%. And it will invest more than $100 billion in enforcing the existing tax laws on the books, laws that are increasingly ignored as the IRS has too few agents to conduct audits of large accounts.

Senate Democrats passed the measure by using the process of budget reconciliation, which covers certain revenue measures and which cannot be filibustered. Although the pieces of the measure have bipartisan support in the country, every Republican voted against the bill; Senate minority leader Mitch McConnell (R-KY) called it an "economic disaster" that will exacerbate inflation (the nonpartisan Congressional Budget Office disagrees).

2. The Bipartisan Safer Communities Act gun safety law.

This is the most significant gun legislation in 30 years. It was passed in response to the multiple mass shootings.

For 2021:

3. The American Rescue Plan Act and extending existing Covid-19 programs.

This series of measures – which make up one of the most consequential pieces of legislation in decades intended to bolster the US' recovery from the coronavirus pandemic – included stimulus payments of up to $1,400 per person for about 90% of American households, a $300 federal boost to weekly jobless benefits and an expansion of the child tax credit of up to $3,600 per child.

The plan, which did not receive support from any Republicans in Congress, also includes $350 billion in state and local aid, as well as billions of dollars for K-12 schools to help students return to the classroom, to assist small businesses hit hard by the pandemic and for vaccine research, development and distribution.

He signed legislation into law extending the Paycheck Protection Program – the federal government's key relief effort to deliver aid to small businesses hard hit by the pandemic. He also signed through the COVID-19 Bankruptcy Relief Extension Act, which extended temporary bankruptcy relief provisions granted by the CARES Act.

4. Infrastructure Investment and Jobs Act

This law infuses $1.2 trillion dollars into Americans' traditional "hard" infrastructure, such as roads and bridges.

NOT ALL CONSTITUTIONAL ACTIVISM IS BAD FOR CONSERVATIVES.

Just the other day, I came across an article about another recently appointed conservative jurist who promised to interpret the law "as written." My first reaction was what judge in his or her right mind would promise to interpret the law as he or she wishes, or unwritten?

But as I thought about this, another more profound issue arose: the promise of conservative legislators to appoint conservative jurists who in turn promise to interpret the Constitution and laws as written—a slap at liberal activists who conservatives say make up theories not in the written law.

Conservative jurists brand themselves as originalists or textualists. Originalists search for the Constitution's original intent or original meaning; that is, they believe the Constitution must be interpreted based on what its drafters originally intended when they wrote it; textualists ask themselves what the words and phrases meant when a particular constitutional provision was adopted.

Originalists believe the Constitution is to be interpreted based on its original meaning—not necessarily what the Founders intended, but how the words they used would have generally been understood at the time.

Both textualists and originalists contend that the Constitution has permanent, static meaning that's baked into it. Both theories are in direct contravention of the "Living Constitution" theory relied on by liberal jurists who believe the Constitution is to be interpreted by considering contemporaneous standards.

A search for the words textualism, textualist, originalism or originalist in the Constitution is a waste of time. They are not there.

Similarly, legal scholars and others needn't bother to search the Constitution to find "executive privilege," or even try to find out how these words were used at the time of the

Constitution's adoption. These words aren't there, and this phrase didn't exist when the Constitution was adopted.

Nevertheless, Donald Trump has repeated relied on a claim of executive privilege to avoid having to turn over to Congress papers, records or any tangible evidence regarding his conduct, and the conduct of others, before and during the January 6 attack on the capital. He has also invoked this doctrine to prevent those who worked in his administration (and others) to prevent them from testifying under oath or offering documents subpoenaed by Congress.

The doctrine of executive privilege defines the authority of the president to withhold documents or information in his possession or in the possession of the executive branch from compulsory demand by subpoena from the legislative branch. (This doctrine has been relied on to avoid compulsory demand from the judicial branch as well.)

This doctrine, as well as the congressional oversight doctrine, were fleshed out in Nixon v. U.S. in 1974 when President Nixon attempted to assert executive privilege to prevent the release of secret tapes, transcripts, and meeting memoranda. His loss before a moderate to liberal Court sealed his fate and led to his resignation. The Constitution is silent on both of these judicially-created doctrines.

The irony here is that Trump asked the Supreme Court justices, a majority of whom are originalists or textualists—again terms not in the Constitution—to grant him freedom from congressional subpoenas based on a doctrine also not mentioned in the Constitution. Further, The authority for the congressional subpoena—congressional oversight—also isn't provided for in the Constitution.

Textualism, Originalism, executive privilege, congressional oversight. None of these appear in the Constitution!

The specter of a Republican president, who carried out his promise to appoint conservative jurists, being forced to rely on a doctrine created by the Supreme Court because it's not in the Constitution, is ironic but not atypical. Conservative jurists have relied on activist interpretations to bring about their preconceived notions. Just read the several dissenting opinions issued during the Court's last term that points out occasions where textualists or originalists became activists in order to achieve their desired end.

Executive privilege is considered an implied power based on the separation of powers set out in Article II, which is meant to make sure one branch of government doesn't become all-powerful.

Presidents have sought to use executive privilege as an absolute shield against Congressional subpoenas involve documentary requests.

But in the case of Donald Trump, it's a situation where a conservative president is relying on an activist doctrine not in the Constitution pitched to conservative justices whose interpretive methods are not in the Constitution.

I suppose Trump believes that not all activist Supreme Court decisions are bad. He just loves the one on executive privilege. Perhaps more than Congress loves its oversight powers---not mentioned in the Constitution.

WHAT GOES AROUND, COMES AROUND

After the FBI raided Trump's Mar-a-Lago, he and his loyalists called the raid un-American and railed about the "weaponization" of the Justice Department. Apart from the whines, moans and groans, it is certainly American to investigate for crimes.

In this case, the improper removal of records at the end of his presidential term is a potential violation of the Presidential Records Act as well as laws about the handling of classified materials. Flushing documents down the toilet certainly is not something presidents do.

What is un-American is lying about election results and setting off an angry mob to stay in power illegally. Trump also had no difficulty trying to weaponize the Justice Department by purging non-loyalists.

What goes around, comes around.

AMERICA A "BANANA REPUBLIC?" SHAME ON THE FINGER-POINTERS!

What does it say about the well-being of our country when well-educated public officials compare America to a "banana republic" for investigating according to the Constitution and laws passed by Congress?

Sen. Ted Cruz is a graduate of Harvard and Princeton. Gov. Ron DeSantis is a graduate of Harvard and Yale. Presumably they, and others similarly educated, are familiar with how investigations are conducted under our system. Law school graduates certainly are presumed to understand this.

First, a person is asked to provide information voluntarily. Failing of that, the government can issue a subpoena. Failing of that, the government can conduct a search and seizure upon a probable cause affidavit demonstrating to a judge that there is probable cause to believe a crime has been committed. This is all the more necessary if there is probable cause to believe potential evidence has been, or could be destroyed, such as by flushing documents down the toilet.

Cruz, DeSantis and others like them know this. They evidently have no trouble when raids are conducted on others when lesser methods have failed; but when the subject of the raid is He Who Must Not Be Investigated, the One Who Is Above the Law, it's an entirely different matter.

Instead of letting the system perform according to its long-standing tradition, we see threats against the judge who issued the subpoena, against the FBI for conducting the raid, the Department of Justice for approving the raid, and threats against anyone who dares to try to hold The Perfect One accountable.

"Defund the FBI." "Impeach Merrick Garland." "Investigate the entire FBI." These are just three of the nonsensical statements being screamed by the outraged.

Instead of trying to calm passions, Cruz, DeSantis and their kind would rather stoke anger and cause their followers to threaten revenge, all because they believe that one man is above the law, and beyond reproach.

What the government is doing is demonstrating how the rule of law works.

What the "banana republic" ranters are doing is undermining our democratic institutions. This raises a far more ominous comparison, the Third Reich.

DONALD TRUMP, WHO REFUSED TO TESTIFY UNDER OATH, RAILS AGAINST THOSE WHO DID.

The FBI raid was in response to Trump's repeated refusal to honor subpoenas, or respond voluntarily. To get a search warrant, the FBI had to demonstrate probable cause that a crime has been committed to a federal judge. This is how our criminal justice system operates under our Constitution. This is a major tenet of what the rule of law means.

This "Banana Republic" nonsense being spewed by Trump's cohorts is designed to keep the party's base agitated.

Trump would have us believe that the many witnesses who testified under oath either lied or made up their testimony, and that only he, who refuses to do the same, is telling the truth.. The only ones who believe this are those willing to be fooled. I don't recall the Republicans suing a single witness for perjury. With good reason: they all told the truth.

Make no mistake about it, Trump believes he is above the law---as do his loyalists. They are about to find out the harsh lesson that he is not, and neither are they.

As Trump said, if you have nothing to hide, why avoid a subpoena, and why plead the Fifth Amendment instead of testifying truthfully under oath? The answer to his own question is obvious: he has plenty to hide, and he can't handle the truth.

THE THIRD OF THREE TRUMPGATES: WHY WOULD TRUMP REMOVE CLASSIFIED RECORDS ABOUT NUCLEAR WEAPONS?

Evidently, the documents sought by the FBI in its authorized raid on Donald Trump's residence relates to classified records about nuclear weapons.

If this is true, several logical questions arise: why would he remove these documents from the White House and place them in his home? What possible benefit is it to him to possess these records, and what plan, if any, does he have regarding those records? Does he have a plan to make them available and, if so, to whom?

These, and no doubt other questions will be asked. They beg for truthful answers under oath

In the meantime, how much of the FBI's search warrant will be disclosed? There may well be classified information in the warrant itself that can't be disclosed.

Assuming what is ultimately disclosed doesn't satisfy Trump, who wants to disclose information that might be classified? Will he disclose classified information in the warrant in defiance of the Department of Justice or the court?

Hopefully, it won't come to that. Hopefully, the complete warrant will be made public for all to see.

This is yet another situation that is unprecedented in an unprecedented presidency: no president has ever removed classified documents from the White House to his home.

By my count, this is Trumpgate number 3. The first Trumpgate was his "perfect" phone call to the Ukraine president for dirt on Hunter Biden in return for release of congressionally approved funds, which led to his first impeachment. Trumpgate number 2 was his instigation of a mob attack on the nation's capital on January 6, 2021, to keep himself in office illegally, which led to his second impeachment. We don't know what the outcome of Trumpgate number 3 will be.

Trump has certainly outdone Richard Nixon. He had one Watergate; Trump has three Trumpgates---so far.

This latest action is just another sad chapter in a book of sad chapters that is the Trump presidency.

IF THE PRESIDENT DOES IT, IT'S LEGAL. DIDN'T WORK FOR NIXON, AND IT WON'T WORK FOR TRUMP

Remember Richard Nixon's early defense of Watergate? If the president does it, it's legal. Look where that got him.

Now, some Trump loyalists are humming the same tune.

It won't work this time either.

Since Trump left office more than 18 months ago, he has had possession, custody and control of all those top secret and other sensitive presidential records.

What has he done with them? Has he made copies? If so, were they given to anyone?

If so, to whom and why?

Was he planning to exchange them for something of value to him? Was he planning on selling them?

Did he make copies, and has he already sold or exchanged them, keeping only the originals? If so, to whom? We know Trump has been friendly to Putin and his buddy from North Korea, among other authoritarians/dictators.

Did he seek advice and counsel in this endeavor? If so, from whom? Who else was aware of his actions, and why have they remained silent? Does this have anything to do with resisting subpoenas and seeking pardons?

Investigators are looking into possible espionage, among other charges of the most serious and severe nature. That means spying. That means treason.

It doesn't get any more serious than that because it puts the security of our nation and our fundamental democratic institutions at risk--in fact, at great peril.

This is not a partisan political hit job. This is not legitimate political discourse. This is not fake news. This is not a liberal media attack--or anything else that the Republican Party's extreme right wing can conjure up to deflect from Trump's own deliberate conduct.

The ultimate question that is rising to the surface should be unthinkable in America, but it must be asked: is the former president of the United States a traitor?

We can only hope and pray he isn't, and that there is a plausible, logical, rational, common-sense reason for taking these records from the White House and secreting them in his home.

DO QUALIFICATIONS FOR PUBLIC OFFICE MATTER ANYMORE?

Considering the trend over the past few years, I wonder if qualifications and merit really matter anymore. It seems that ideology and cult loyalty are becoming more and more important.

If qualifications mattered, those members of the House who voted to impeach Trump would have defeated those whose only qualification is loyalty to Trump. We wouldn't have mental gnats like Taylor Greene, Boebert and their ilk wreaking havoc with our form of government. I like political figures who clearly state what they're for, how they plan to implement their ideas, and how those ideas will benefit all of us.

Don't give me platitudes, buzzwords and BS; and don't tell me what you're against. Tell me why you're better on the substantive issues than your opponent(s). Make your case not by running down your opposition, but by showing how you will make things better. But perhaps I seek too much.

THE REAL EXISTENTIAL THREAT

Here is the nub of the threat to our nation represented by the extremists that have captured the Republican Party: it is perfectly proper to "weaponize" the government to go after Hillary Clinton and other designated enemies, but it is criminal to go after Trump for admittedly taking classified, highly sensitive records and storing them in his home. And if he says he declassified records on nuclear weapons, that's ok, too.

For daring to investigate Trump for possible espionage (we don't yet know who accessed those records), the party leaders want to destroy the FBI and threaten public officers and officials with acts of violence.

And tens of millions, including party leaders, have no problem with any of this.

Those in charge of taking care that the laws be faithfully executed and obligated to uphold the rule of law must not be intimidated by this nonsense.

If you do the crime, you must do the time.

IS THIS WHAT THE REPUBICAN PARTY MEANS BY LAW AND ORDER?

Martin Hyde, a businessman and Republican candidate for the United States House of Representatives in Florida has said he would have sent FBI agents home "in a body bag" if they had raided his home the way they searched Mar-a-Lago.

We know Donald Trump wants to remake the party in his own image, but the question must be asked: Is this the kind of candidate the Republican Party wants to elect to Congress and other public office?

This is beyond outrageous; yet where is the outrage from the party itself? This nut is saying that had he taken property illegally and the FBI came to his home with a search warrant based on probable cause, he would shoot the agents.

Is this the party's new definition of law and order? This is sheer madness, yet it's become almost mainstream due to public officials who should know better accusing the FBI of acting like a banana republic, or worse.

This is not rational; this is not sanity. This is dangerous because it condones violence against the legitimate exercise of law and order under our Constitution and statutes. This guy favors taking the law into one's own hands, the only basis being an "I don't like it" mentality that in his warped mind, justifies the most violent of crimes. We can only hope that sanity returns to the Republican Party before it's too late.

WHY DO PEOPLE VOTE AGAINST THEIR OWN INTERESTS?

As we approach the 2022 election cycle, this question arises: why do so many people vote against their own interests? Social security and Medicare are prime examples of millions of people doing precisely that.

Today, approximately 69 million Americans receive Social Security; approximate 64 million are on Medicare. The party split is about even, so roughly 34.5 million Republicans receive social security checks and 32 million receive Medicare benefits. Both programs were passed and became law during the Democratic administrations of Franklin Roosevelt and Lyndon Johnson. Therefore, it is a matter of fact that Republicans benefit from a program started by the Democrats in response to the economic meltdown of the late 1920s and medical care conditions in the 1950s to mid-1960s.

Yet, today's Republican Party wants to scrap both programs as we know it. At least two leading Republican senators support upending both of these programs.

Florida Sen. Rick Scott said he wants to tax Social Security benefits. Sen. Ron Johnson of Wisconsin suggested that Social Security and Medicare be transformed into programs whose budgets are annually appropriated by Congress. Most House Republicans agree with him.

The Republican Study Committee, which represents 157 out of 211 House Republicans, holds slashing Medicare and Social Security as a core tenant of their proposed budget.

There is even talk amongst Republicans of privatizing both programs. Imagine that, turning both programs over to the ancestors of those whose policies and actions led to Black Friday in 1929 and the ensuing Great Depression, and the Great Recession of 2008! Yet, millions of Republican recipients are prepared to vote for their party faithful—and even try to increase their number in Congress—and by doing so, vote for those who want to upend these two essential programs that provide them with vital benefits.

This is a classic example of voting against one's own best interests. How does putting Social Security and Medicare on the congressional chopping block every year help those in the working class whose daily efforts bring them closer and closer to the day of their retirement? Clearly, it doesn't.

There was a time when people who were no longer able to work either because of age or infirmity were shunted off to the sidelines with no economic security, except perhaps for those who invested in companies, including those that eventually collapsed. Does today's version of the Republican Party want to take us back to that era? Keep reading.

Social Security and Medicare aren't the only lifesaving programs the GOP is gunning for. MSNBC's Steve Benen set out clearly what would happen if House Republicans' budgetary plan were to come to fruition:

"Social Security and Medicare would be partially privatized, food stamps would be slashed, Head Start would be phased out, Medicaid funding would be decimated, the Affordable Care Act would be weakened, labor unions would be undermined, the EPA would be gutted, abortion would be banned [a goal already accomplished], birthright citizenship would be eliminated, Donald Trump's border wall would be funded, and even the Consumer Financial Protection Bureau would see its doors permanently closed."

In Florida, its governor and wannabee president Ron DeSantis wants to change the state's well-performing pension fund by prohibiting the state from considering what are known as environmental, social governance (ESG) standards when investing state money in companies. ESG is a 20-year-old movement to encourage corporate responsibility by encouraging investment in companies that have policies addressing issues like climate change, human rights and racial injustice.

I suppose that the old adage "if it ain't broke, don't fix it" no longer applies to the current version of the Republican Party. It should be abundantly clear that today's Republican Party wants to take us back to the 1920s when the policies of three consecutive Republican presidents drove our economy over the cliff in 1929. Closer in time, the conservatives want to take us back to the eight years of George Bush II economic policies that led to the economic meltdown in 2008, the "too big to fail" era.

Imagine that! Today's Republican Party, which having been captured by the far-right wing is but a shell of what it was back then, wants to return to policies that drove our economy over the cliff, which has happened twice in the last 100 years as a result of their past economic policies. You would think the party would want to avoid a repeat of its economic failures.

But the party's theme now is "if you can't read about it, or learn about it in school, it didn't happen." This "head in the sand" attitude toward education is the sine qua non or essential element of tragedy borne of ignorance. Republicans are mandating what schools, colleges and universities can and, more importantly, can't teach, and telling Americans what they can and can't read or say. Ignorance of the past means the tragedy of repetition. But, party faithful say, voting blue means higher taxes and more crime, and that voting red will reduce taxes and crime.

Wanting to tax social security benefits means higher taxes for 69 million Americans, including 34 million Republicans. And those tax cuts of 2017 are permanent only for the wealthy; tax cuts for the middle class are set to expire in 2025, when the Republican Party hopes to have control of

Congress and the White House, and a compliant Supreme Court.

And with Republicans in charge in Washington and Florida, crime hasn't exactly plummeted to historic low depths. If the old song about the rich getting richer and the poor getting poorer rings true, what do you think will happen to the crime rate as more and more reach poverty level under oppressive economic policies like those of past Republican administrations?

Imagine what the party will do to those programs that benefit the majority of Americans, and a majority of Americans favor, according to latest polls. The party leadership's response seems to be: a pox on those polls, we know better. And their voters go merrily along, once again demonstrating how voters vote against their own interests.

There is one overriding reason why people vote against their own interests: fear. If you can create enough fear of the "other side," people will vote against "those evildoers" without focusing on--or even caring about--the effects of their vote on themselves. Whether it's ignorance or indifference doesn't matter; it's only whether the goal is reached. As Joseph Goebbels noted many years ago, this is the ultimate value of propaganda and thought control.

IN HIS LATEST EFFORT TO AVOID HIS DAY OF RECONING, TRUMP WANTS A FEDERAL SPECIAL MASTER TO REVIEW HIS MAR-A-LAGO RECORDS

This is the latest in Donald Trump's arsenal of delaying tactics. What he is seeking is what a federal magistrate usually does.

Of the five reasons justifying the appointment by a federal judge of a special master, only two might be relevant: the existence of some exceptional condition; or to address pretrial matters that can't be effectively and timely addressed by an available district judge or district magistrate judge.

The only possible exceptional condition is that the matter involves a former president of the United States. Federal judges issue search warrants based on probable cause affidavits by the bucketsful every day. While the raid is unprecedented, it's based on Trump's conduct which is also unprecedented in American history. Trump wants special treatment because of who he is, not what he did.

The second justification is flawed because if the issue involves an issue that will take an extraordinary amount of time, the presiding judge will usually hand the matter to a magistrate judge whose job it is to perform the task. Usually, matters pertaining to pretrial discovery are presided over by a magistrate judge. In Trump's case, there is no pretrial matter at issue because there is no case that is moving toward trial.

Of course, any special master not of Trump's liking will allow him to further claim prejudice, or that the process is a hoax, or any other the other nonsensical reasons that his loyalists buy while allowing for further dilatory actions.

Typically, an appointed special master is a highly regarded lawyer who understands the rules of evidence and can deal effectively and relatively quickly with these types of issues.

If the court is of a mind to appoint a special master to appease Trump, there are certainly prominent lawyers with deep Republican credentials. Robert Mueller and James Comey come to mind.

THIS IS NOT LEADERSHIP

According to Center for Disease Control data reported this month by the U.S. News and World Report, among all 50 states, Florida has the second highest percentage of counties with a high community level of COVID prevalence as determined by the number of new COVID cases and hospitalizations. Another study reveals that Florida has the third highest number of reported monkeypox cases in America.

Yet not a word about this from Gov. Ron DeSantis, or his loyalists. Their attitude seems to be if you don't hear about it, or don't read about it, it didn't happen or it's not happening.

This is a grave threat to our democracy because "Democracy dies in darkness," as the Washington Post aptly notes. This recognizes that a democracy can't survive and thrive without an electorate informed with facts and truth by a free and independent press.

This is a classic case of leadership by ideology—someone who's too busy waging a culture war to engage and address real substantive problems affecting real people. Florida ranks 22nd in the total number of those who've had at least one vaccination; the state has the fifth lowest among the states in reported vaccinations for children under five. Again, not a word from DeSantis in dealing with significant issues affecting our state's health and well-being.

DeSantis is defining his leadership skills by the number of people he can anger by his "anti-woke" rants, either ignoring or not knowing that woke means "aware of and actively attentive to important facts and issues (especially issues of racial and social justice)." He wants his constituents to be ignorant of these issues. That's precisely what being anti-woke means. What he's done is convert knowledge and information into an epithet.

But that's not all; he has also been very busy cleansing education curriculum, banning books, changing voting laws under a bogus claim of fraud, and punishing anyone and everyone who dares to disagree with him.

This type of leadership is more along the lines of the despot, who arouses anger which eventually leads to hatred.

History is replete with those who led by authoritarianism, creating an "us vs. them" environment. History tells us of the evil they created, the needless loss of life, and their ultimate dumping in history's garbage bin.

Leadership is Franklin Roosevelt, Theodore Roosevelt, Harry Truman, etc. I would add Winston Churchill to this list. They dealt with the great social and economic issues of their time. They didn't engage in culture wars or create an "us vs. them" mentality stoked by anger and resentment. These leaders recognized societal conditions and worked diligently to address them through prudent policies that historians cite to show what real leadership is.

I can remember a time when Florida had statesmen at its helm. People like LeRoy Collins, Reuben Askew, Lawton Chiles, Bob Graham, Claude Pepper, etc. Now, we have Rick Scott—he of questionable business practices who hid behind the Fifth Amendment numerous times before being elected governor, and who now wants to tax or privatize social security. We also have Marco Rubio—he who looks more like "little boy lost" than a United States senator, and is AWOL on too many occasions.

And we have Ron DeSantis, certainly more charismatic than these two senators, but that's not really saying much. DeSantis is a lot smarter and more charismatic than Donald Trump, but that's not saying much, either. And he doesn't have Trump's baggage, which is very appealing to his supporters. You can bet he is just biding his time and carefully positioning himself, waiting for Trump to implode. After all, Trump will be 78 in 2024 and currently faces a heap of legal issues.

What DeSantis is doing is cleverly and without the Trump pity party playing into anger and resentment that had been building for years since the Obama election; emotions that a personality flawed Trump exposed; and the more polished DeSantis stands ready to capitalize on.

It would be not only nice but proper for DeSantis to take those CDC numbers and address all Floridians with a comprehensive plan to deal with these public health issues. But we know that's not going to happen. Instead, it will be up to Charlie Crist to try to get through to the voters that neither ideology nor taking a "head in the sand" approach will address the state's pressing issues of real importance.

We now have a clear idea of how DeSantis will lead should he run for and be elected president. A very clear idea.

History will not be kind to the current Florida leadership.

SOME THOUGHTS ON PRESIDENT BIDEN'S FORGIVENESS OF STUDENT LOANS

The Biden administration is cancelling up to $10,000 of student debt for millions of people and up to $20,000 of debt for low- and middle-income borrowers who previously received a Pell grant. The loan relief will be limited to borrowers who earn less than $125,000 a year or families earning less than $250,000.

The skyrocketing costs have placed higher education and the opportunities that flow from it beyond the financial ability of much of the middle class, and you can forget about those below the poverty line.

I borrowed $3000 from the federal government to make it through my undergraduate years. It took me 10 years at $30 a month to pay that off. Today, this amount is not even a drop in the bucket. Except for the wealthy, education costs have created a guaranteed mortgage for millions. Try getting though a reputable undergraduate program living away from home for less than $100,000. Even living at home will result in costs of $40,000-$50,000.

And if the goal is graduate school, that's another six-figure loan, and another mortgage. I bet those who flat-out oppose forgiving student loans would feel far differently if they were the ones who had the debt, but that's another story. Maybe this reduction will result in education costs becoming more realistic and reachable for more people. Having said this, however, I'm ambivalent in simply forgiving a part of these loans without something in return from the debtholder. Some of the suggestions for a form of payback like public service have some merit. As with so many federal programs, the devil's in the details.

HERE IS ONE REASON WHY REPUBLICANS DON'T WANT AN INFORMED, AWARE CITIZENRY—THEY CAN ENGAGE IN THIS TYPE OF HYPOCRISY WITHOUT BEING HELD ACCOUNTABLE

There is a long-standing tradition in Congress for its members to boast about their votes that help "bring home the bacon," that is, bring home money to their constituents.

But lately, Republican legislators have been taking credit for the benefits of legislation they opposed on the floor. In short, they are taking credit for what they voted against.

One graphic example of this is the passage of the infrastructure legislation. After the Biden administration announced that the law would provide $1.1 billion to protect and restore the Everglades in South Florida, Sen. Rick Scott said:

"It was good to be with the Army Corps and our strong local leaders today to see the great progress being made at the Herbert Hoover Dike. I was the first governor to dedicate state funding to make the critical repairs to the Herbert Hoover Dike at Lake Okeechobee and am proud that Senator Rubio and I were able to help secure an unprecedented $1 billion for Everglades restoration, the largest single amount ever allocated by the federal government."

There is one problem with this statement: it's not true. Neither Scott nor Marco Rubio voted for the law that included funding for the Everglades protection and restoration program.

These senators—and other Republican members of Congress like them--are hoping their constituents aren't smart or aware enough to see through their charade. and call them out for their lies. Recall that the definition of hypocrisy is saying one thing and doing another.

Whether the legislation involves COVID relief funds or matters addressing climate change and inflation reduction, or any other legislation passed by Democrats that are popular with the public, Republicans are taking credit for legislation they voted against.

This is one sure way to deal with situations where they voted against legislation that enjoys broad public support, albeit a dishonest one. This is especially so when the legislation, passed by a Democratic majority and signed by a Democratic president, provides funds to local governments and is designed to create new jobs and economic growth—points that fit the Republican Party's proffered goals.

A prime example of this occurred after the after the passage last year of the $1.9 trillion American Rescue Plan Act, with its COVID-19 pandemic relief for individuals, businesses and local governments. Not a single Republican supported it; yet, several Republicans later claimed they supported various programs and provisions of the legislation they rejected.

It is to be expected that Republicans will continue with this type of self-praise for programs they oppose as long as their supporters buy it.

Their approach is to rail at the evildoing Democrats while filling their supporters with political compost…and hoping they'll continue to buy it whole hog. And they will, so long as the politicos can keep their constituents unaware of their false statements and angry at the evildoers. In short, so long as their voters don't call them out for their hypocrisy, they'll continue to engage in it.

MORE ABOUT PRESIDENT BIDEN'S STUDENT LOAN FORGIVENESS PLAN

A friend of mine has taken issue with President Biden eliminating a portion of student debt, saying it sends a poor message on personal responsibility to young debtors. Reiterating the typical Republican line, he says It feeds a welfare mentality; entitlement without obligation. By his action on this issue, President Biden is continuing his poor policies of trying to solve every problem by throwing money at it. His timing on this student debt decision is clearly intended to favorably impact primarily the young voters at mid-term.

I answered him in kind. I told him I have a friend whose daughter lived at home and had use of the family car for all three years in law school, yet she owes over $40,000 in loan money. Imagine what that amount would be if she went to another law school in-state or, worse, an out-of-state law school. That would be a six-figure mortgage. And I can only imagine what the average debt for a med student is.

The point is that, through lending institution policies fostered by government, we have created a debtors society. I, too, resent those who game the system by taking out loans and then failing or refusing to pay them back. But I also resent those institutions who have been allowed to create a situation where loan payback itself becomes oppressive.

Take that "mere" $40,000 debt. If paid back at $500 a month, it will take more than 6 years to pay it back. If this student gets a government job, I don't have to tell you what her take home salary will be. How about getting married, buying a home, having and raising a family? Two mortgages. Now, take that same amount and triple or quadruple it. I think you see the problem here. A huge mortgage to start your life.

You say eliminating debt sends a poor message on personal responsibility. But what message is sent when Congress gives huge tax breaks to the wealthy, and bails them out when things go south as happened in 2008? It's called corporate welfare, and it's alive and well in America when the Republicans have control of Congress and the White

House. You are certainly aware that the 2017 tax cuts were made permanent for the wealthy; those for the middle class expire in 2025. The appearance of personal responsibility is a two-edged sword.

And since personal responsibility is such a driving force among Republicans, I would hope this would apply to Donald Trump, his White House loyalists; his congressional lemmings; and others who are on the hook under our criminal laws yet evade subpoenas and plead the Fifth Amendment. What message does this scofflaw behavior send to our youth?

Solving pressing problems long ignored by the Republicans requires spending money. Try fixing roads and bridges without it. Try coming up with vaccines to ward off potentially catastrophic consequences without it. Try to accomplish anything worthwhile without it. The only thing that doesn't cost a lot of money for the Republicans is engaging in a cultural war. That's cheap but draconian, and dangerous to democracy. But that's another story.

It's not a matter of spending money; it's a matter of priorities. The Republicans want to help, aid and assist business--more specifically big business. Their view is that benefits will trickle down to the mass of laborers. This trickle-down approach has been proven bogus over and over again, yet they stick to it because that's where their campaign funds come from. Quid pro quo.

As for Biden's poor policies of throwing money at every problem, that's a great tag line until it's put under a microscope. How would the Republicans try to address our deteriorating infrastructure? They've had Reagan, Bush, Bush II and Trump and we still have a rapidly deteriorating infrastructure. A Republican health plan to replace Obamacare? It doesn't exist and never will. When it comes to actually dealing with issues that affect the majority of Americans, it's all culture talk and no policy action. As for poor policies, just look at conservative America of Harding, Coolidge and Hoover in the 1920s and during the Bush II years to see the consequences of poor economic policies. As for timing, you aren't seriously suggesting that Republicans have never acted to gain approval of voters close to an election.

But it doesn't stop here. Author and historian Heather Cox Richardson has once again disclosed the hypocrisy that runs rampant in the Republican Party.

This time, it's about President Biden's student loan forgiveness plan. Read the outrage of these members of Congress, and see how much they received in loan forgiveness. Here it is:

"After a day of Republican congress members railing against yesterday's educational loan forgiveness of up to $20,000 for Pell Grant recipients and $10,000 for others, the White House tweeted a thread of those members alongside the amount of Paycheck Protection Program (PPP) money those individuals were forgiven.

Representative Marjorie Taylor Greene (R-GA) said: "For our government just to say ok your debt is completely forgiven.. it's completely unfair." Greene had $183,504 in PPP loans forgiven.

Representative Vern Buchanan (R-FL) said: "Biden's reckless, unilateral student loan giveaway is unfair to the 87 percent of Americans without student loan debt and those who played by the rules." Buchanan had more than $2.3 million in PPP loans forgiven.

Representative Markwayne Mullin (R-OK) said: "We do not need farmers and ranchers, small business owners, and teachers in Oklahoma paying the debts of Ivy League lawyers and doctors across the U.S." Mullin had more than $1.4 million in PPP loans forgiven.

Representative Kevin Hern (R-OK) said: "To recap, in the last two weeks, the 'Party of the People' has supercharged the IRS to go after working-class Americans, raised their taxes, and forced them to pay for other people's college degrees." Hern had more than $1 million in PPP loans forgiven.

Representative Mike Kelly (R-PA) said: "Asking plumbers and carpenters to pay off the loans of Wall Street advisors and lawyers isn't just unfair. It's also bad policy." Kelly had $987,237 in PPP loans forgiven.

Representative Matt Gaetz (R-FL) said: Everyone knows that in a $60 Billion+ European land war, it's always the last $3 Billion that kicks in the door…." Gaetz had $482,321 in PPP loans forgiven."

Their brand should be "We are Republicans and we are shameless."

Remember, when you point a finger at the other side, you have three fingers pointing at you.

DONALD TRUMP'S PITY PARTY: HE HAS NO ONE TO BLAME BUT HIMSELF

Donald Trump is feeding his loyalists the line that he's the most persecuted president in American history. As his crowd of adoring admirers cheer in agreement, he adds that if he were to withdraw as a presidential candidate in 2024, all of the persecution would stop.

Of course, there is no way to prove the latter, unless he actually does withdraw—which we all know he's not going to do. But it is a remarkable ploy to keep his faithful cultists in his corner.

Whether he is the most persecuted president in our nation's history is quite beside the point. He's on course to become the first prosecuted president in history.

But the question that must be asked when he lavishes his mindless minions with his pity party "oh, woe is me" routine is what is the cause of his distress?

The answer is obvious to all with an open mind who can see the trees through the forest he's created.

The cause of his distress, the source of his predicament, is Donald Trump.

As the saying goes, he made his bed, now he must sleep in it.

No one forced Trump to diss our nation's allies as he did both before and during his term.

No one forced him to attempt to seriously weaken NATO by threatening to withdraw our nation from our critical alliance against aggressive threats from foreign sources.

No one made him give aid and comfort to hate groups that espouse anti-minority, anti-Black and anti-Semitic rhetoric.

No one made him do all but kiss Russian despot Vladimir Putin's ring during that infamous meeting in Helsinki, Finland in 2018. You may recall that our national intelligence agencies unanimously concluded that Russia played a role in influencing the outcome of the 2016 election in favor of Trump. After Putin denied his country's involvement, Trump said he believed Putin over our own government agencies. His chance to confront our greatest adversary turned into a fawning exhibition showing great weakness where strength was required. With Trump doing Putin's work by attempting to weaken NATO and undercut our allies, Putin had everything he ever wanted from Trump.

No one compelled him to call the president of Ukraine during the run-up to the 2020 presidential election seeking political dirt on President Biden's son in exchange for release of congressionally appropriated funds. This quid pro quo "perfect" phone call—the transcript of which Trump himself released—led to his first impeachment, and only his genuflecting supporters in the Senate saved him from removal from office.

No one forced Trump, who avoided military service by citing a bone spur in his foot, to disparage veterans who were wounded or captured or went missing in action by calling them "losers" and "suckers."

No one compelled him to lie repeatedly about the 2020 election results that eventually led to the attack by his easily persuaded loyalists—made up largely of hate groups—on our nation's capital in America's latest day of infamy, January 6, 2021. This attack resulted in five deaths and injuries to more than 140 law enforcement officers. This, by the leader of the party that claims to have cornered the market on law and order. This attack led to his second impeachment and, once again, his senate cronies gave him a pass.

We continue to learn more and more of his actions, and those of his White House staff, that show Trump's knowledge and conduct from the November election to January 6, and it isn't pretty for him or our nation. The testimony and evidence before the House select committee investigating that attack that is damning of Trump's behavior has come from Republicans, including those who worked near him in the White House. It doesn't get more damning than that.

Trump knew the truth of the election outcome, but his massive ego prevented him from accepting it. So he conjured up a lie, repeated it, his true believers believed it, and are still living with the sad, tragic consequences of his own creation.

No one forced Trump to illegally remove dozens of boxes and hundreds of pages of classified documents from the White House to his private residence. This is a clear violation of federal law. Since Trump isn't talking under oath—and won't unless he's faced with no other choice—we can only wonder who has seen those highly sensitive records involving nuclear weapons and other top-secret documents.

And then there are those cases still pending in various courts regarding his questionable business and financial dealings over many years. No one made him engage in those shady practices. You would think that the illegal practices of Trump University—the number of individuals who were conned into his program only to be taken advantage of--would have given voters a sense of what to expect from a Trump presidency, but as the saying goes, there are none so blind as he who will not see.

In each instance noted here—and they are certainly not all inclusive—Trump has attempted to portray himself as the victim. That's the authoritarian mindset: blame others for the problems you've created.

Trump will no doubt continue with his rallies, repeating his pity party woes to his idol worshippers. They will believe what he says because he has mesmerized them into believing everything he says and does. He is their fount of wisdom, truth and righteousness. But he fools only them; he doesn't fool the tens of millions who see through his act.

Trump is a seriously flawed man. His behavior is that of a malignant narcissist. He appears juvenile in his mannerisms and speech patterns. In his mind, he is "perfect," incapable of doing wrong. He trusts his gut over his own educated and trained advisors. And on and on and on. His niece, Mary Trump, wrote a book about her uncle's flawed psychological makeup. His words and deeds are out there for all to see.

Trump is a victim alright. He is a victim of Donald Trump. His greatest enemy is Donald Trump. He has no one to blame but himself.

THE TRUMP REDACTED SEARCH WARRANT AFFIDAVIT; RECALL THE REDACTED MUELLER REPORT

For those of you who've read the Mueller Report with its multiple redactions, wait until you cast your eyes on the redacted Trump search warrant affidavit that is about to be released.

This is the affidavit that has been redacted by the FBI and approved for release by the federal magistrate. I think it's safe to say that those looking for revelations will be most disappointed. There might be some general information, but I doubt there will be anything of a revelatory nature. Recall the Department of Justice opposed releasing any part of the affidavit to "protect the integrity of an ongoing law enforcement investigation that implicates national security," noting that the disclosure would lead to "inevitable efforts to read between the lines and discern the identities of certain individuals, dates, or other critical, case-specific information,"

Finally, the DOJ maintained that it isn't possible to make a redacted version of the affidavit public because the redactions would be "so extensive as to render the document devoid of content that would meaningfully enhance the public's understanding of these events."

The judge nevertheless accepted the redacted version and ordered its release in its fully redacted form. Re-read the last quoted paragraph, and you get a solid picture of what we're about to see. Sure enough, the redacted affidavit explains why the search was necessary, but the details as described above were redacted.

THE FEARMONGERING OF "TAX AND SPEND"

Well, it's campaign time once again, and the Republicans are sharpening their slogans to arouse their masses. And their sloganeering works—so long as the masses don't look behind their rage for facts. The reason for this: the facts aren't there.

Let's look at one such slogan: tax and spend. Repeated often enough by Republican officeholders and candidates, it allows the adoring masses to simply repeat it as if it shows great knowledge and intelligence about what the Democrats are all about. Actually, to the informed, it shows neither.

Those who hook onto the elephant's tail and see that very large object in front of them won't ask these questions, so here they are: who is being taxed, and what is being spent?

The Democrats have been trying to tax the super wealthy and mega corporations for years, believing they should pay their fair share. Of course, this is anathema to the Republicans, who look to these rich sources for contributions, donations and other benefits in return for the great tax and business windfalls they get that aren't available to the rest of us.

Let's separate the two. Here are the facts regarding the taxing part.

For individuals, the Biden administration proposals are designed to avoid increasing taxes on individuals with annual incomes below $400,000; to create benefits, largely in the form of refundable tax credits, such as the already enacted earned income and child tax credits, for the poor and those with low and moderate incomes; and to target any tax increases for the wealthy. Of course, the benefits mentioned here flow to Republicans as well as everyone one else. But Republicans will never admit to gaining benefits from Democratic-passed legislation. They will, instead, hypocritically take credit for legislation they opposed that happen to benefit their constituents.

For the wealthy, the Biden administration's proposed top income tax rate would increase the present law's 37% rate to 39.6%. This increase will affect only the top 1% of taxpayers. The new top federal tax rate on capital gains would total 43.4%, almost double the top combined rate of 23.8% under present law.

Biden administration representatives indicate that only taxpayers whose incomes exceed $1 million would be subject to the higher tax on capital gains. However, it is not clear if the $1 million threshold would apply per individual taxpayer or per return; on a per-individual basis, the threshold for a joint return would be $2 million.

Tax law is a separate and complicated field of law, but the essential elements of what is proposed affects very few individuals; the target is the wealthy who have been blessed with great benefits but have not been paying their fair share.

But these basic facts get lost when the purpose of the Republican mantra is to create enough fog that their masses can't see through it.

Now here's the spending part.

The next time you drive over a large pothole and get angry over the lack of repair, or drive over a rusted-out bridge wondering if the cars following you will be as lucky, ask yourself how those roads and bridges get repaired. Do you think some genie shows up as if by magic and begins to make repairs on roads, bridges and other infrastructure that have been neglected for too long?

The next time you have a power outage due to deteriorating utility lines and transformers, ask yourself how these parts of our infrastructure will be repaired. Do you believe it's done by simply snapping your fingers?

The next time you read about unprecedented fires raging out west, or flooded roads and streets in the south- and mid-west (and elsewhere), which are destroying homes, businesses, upending lives, etc., ask yourself how these climate change conditions can be alleviated. Again, do you think some magician is going to solve these wide-ranging problems for free?

Face reality. These repairs and maintenance cost money. It takes money to hire the people to make these and other long-neglected repairs. Whether employed by government or the private sector, it takes trained people with proper supplies and equipment to make the needed repairs and to maintain them in proper working condition over the years. Substantively addressing climate change takes money. There is no free lunch here.

Here's another reality. If you buy cheap, you get cheap. Would you want to fly cross-country on an old prop or a modern jet? It's the same question regarding infrastructure and climate change. Quality is more important than trying to squeeze juice out of a penny. Buying less than top quality will cost more in the long run by necessitating more frequent repairs and replacements. Band-aids are useless.

Providing the funds necessary to address infrastructure and climate change could have been accomplished earlier, but Republican intransigence prevented action. And they would have continued to block action if they had their way. They would have spent more time crying their "tax and spend" tears while finding additional windfalls for the wealthy.

But "tax and spend" sounds good to the gullible masses, and for Republican officeholders and those seeking office, it works.

Fortunately, the Democrats didn't buy into the bogus "tax and spend" label. Instead, they chose to do what has been needed for so very long—pass legislation that deals with pressing nationwide problems that can't be kicked down the road any longer.

THE SEARCH WARRANT AFFIDAVIT RAISES THE UGLIEST OF QUESTIONS ABOUT TRUMP'S CONDUCT

We know that some of the top-secret information stored in Donald Trump's home and resort pertain to nuclear weapons. There is certainly other top secret, highly sensitive classified information he stored there as well since he left the White House more than 18 months ago. Since the search of Donald Trump's residence and resort, and the release of the redacted affidavit supporting the judicially issued search warrant, the penultimate question that author and historian Heather Cox Richardson is now asking is who else has seen those documents? Who else knows what no average American knows?

As she notes in her column yesterday:

"This stolen and mishandled classified intelligence compromises our security. The best-case scenario is that it was never seen by anyone who knew what they were looking at. Even that would mean that our allies have every reason to be leery about sharing information with us again.

But that's the best-case scenario. We have to wonder, who else now knows the secrets designed to keep Americans safe? Multiple news stories during Trump's presidency noted that even then, Mar-a-Lago was notoriously insecure. And, unthinkable though it should be but sadly is not, what if secret documents have already been given or sold into the hands of foreign actors whose interests conflict with ours?"

The question posed here must be answered. Americans need to know their security is being protected, not compromised. Trump is well-known for engaging in a sympathy campaign. In his mind, he's done no wrong. He's the epitome of human perfection. He's misunderstood. He is the most victimized person in human history. What he really is is a danger to America.

In his feckless defense, he says he declassified all this information. But that only begs the obvious question: why would he declassify such top-secret information? What possible purpose would it serve for him to do that? We know from his past that he craves money. He's constantly searching for ways to increase his wealth. We don't know what kind of debt he is carrying, but from all the lawsuits he's filed--and continues to file---we can easily surmise that he needs cash.

We also know of his cozy relationships with his buddy in Moscow, and his newfound friend in North Korea. As Richardson profoundly asks: have those secret records "already been given or sold into the hands of foreign actors whose interests conflict with ours?" Knowing Trump's past,

I would bet on sale if those records were in fact placed in the hands of others.

If Richardson is asking these questions, you can bet others are as well. Others such as members of Congress who are faithful to their oaths to protect the United States from all enemies, foreign and domestic--the oath Trump and his congressional loyalists evidently have forgotten.

We can only contemplate the consequences of those records in the hands of someone with no moral compass falling into the hands of others with no moral compass.

Years ago, when Hillary Clinton used her private email server to conduct government business, those on the far right accused her of treason. Despite the Republican Party having control of Congress and the White House (and the entire prosecutorial arm of the federal government), not a single charge was ever filed against her. There is one simple reason: they never had a case against her. Richardson doesn't use that ugly word, but if the answer to her "unthinkable" question is that Trump did share those records, then that ugly word has profound relevance.

QUESTIONS TO PONDER REGARDING THE RELEASE OF A REDACTED VERSION OF THE TRUMP AFFIDAVIT

Michael Conway, former counsel to the House Judiciary Committee, explains why no part of the Mar-a-Lago affidavit should have been disclosed. For his reasoning, he accepts the Department of Justice's position that disclosure of any part could lead to the identification of those involved in preparing the affidavit and any underlying information, identify witnesses and compromise this, as well as future, investigations.

But there are other considerations as well. Using this as precedent, what would prevent any public official or public person subject to a search from demanding that the warrant-supporting affidavit be disclosed? In fact, what would prevent any person served with a search warrant from demanding the same treatment?

Well, it might be said, this was an unprecedented search of a former president's abode. But what about that language that says that everyone is treated equally under the law, that the law recognizes no special treatment or favor, and that no person is above the law?

It is certainly true that the subject of this search warrant, and the items searched, are unprecedented. But does that alone justify disparate treatment under our system of justice that's supposed to be blind?

Search warrants are issued upon probable cause affidavits every day. This is a usual, commonplace procedure. Likewise, nondisclosure of this information is the norm, especially early on in a potential criminal proceeding. The Trump warrant is an early stage in the process.

In this instance, releasing a redacted version opens up the investigation to conspiracy theorists and others who will read what they want into the blacked out lines.

Historically, we are a nation that abhors secrecy, even with evolving technology that implicates secrecy's very foundation. We also cherish privacy, even though through technology and government actions, that has taken a hit.

But those in charge of preserving our democracy well know that some things must be kept secret in the interests of national security.

As we move forward from this precedent-setting judicial action, it is wise to keep in mind how this will affect the administration of our criminal justice system in the future.

"I FEAR FOR THE COUNTRY."

Vermont Sen. Patrick Leahy, who is retiring at the end of this year as the third longest serving senator in American history, was asked about the prospects of Donald Trump being indicted for crimes.

"I fear for the country. Because what they're saying is, if you do anything that disagrees with Trump, there's a target on your back. There are people working in government who suddenly feel threatened because they dared raise a question. Donald Trump would say how pro-law enforcement they were until law enforcement came after him for breaking the law. Now they're all evil. It makes no sense."

Focus on this for prospect for a moment. The nation's criminal justice system, forged by our Constitution and almost 250 years of trial and error that is our democracy, functioning based on fear.

Leahy has been around a long time. He's the president pro tempore of the senate, completing his eighth term, and was a Vermont state prosecutor for eight years before that. He has seen it all, yet he fears for the future because of the level of fear that has been injected into our criminal justice system.

Attorney General Merrick Garland is faced with a decision unprecedented in American history: does the Department of Justice consider indicting a former president based on the law and the facts applied to the law, or based on fear of violent reprisals?

As of a few days ago, about 900 participants in the January 6 attack on the capital have been arrested; over 360 have plead guilty. These numbers are expected to rise as those behind bars begin to talk, leading to more charges, more convictions and more imprisonment.

All of this is being accomplished without fear, based solely on application of facts to the nation's laws.

After the search of Trump's Mar-a-Lago property and seizure of classified documents, one outraged man armed with an AR-15 rifle and a nail gun and wearing body armor, tried to breach the FBI's Cincinnati field office. He paid the ultimate price for his rage. This man had associates within a far-right extremist group, and a social media account seems to have referenced an attempt to storm an FBI office. It also made a "call to arms" – and called for violence against the agency – after the FBI executed a search warrant at Trump's Florida home.

Our nation simply can't survive this kind of madness spread across the country.

To be sure, criticism of judicial decisions, especially those of the Supreme Court, is nothing new. The Court was criticized during the 1930s for upending much of FDR's New Deal. The Court faced strong criticism for its liberal leanings during the 1950s and 1960s. Bush v. Gore led to much criticism in 2000, and its recent abortion decision invoked much rage.

But acts of violence like the one described above is not criticism; it's vigilantism—taking the law into one's own hands. No true American can favor or tolerate such lawlessness and call themselves advocates of law and order, and the rule of law.

You might recall the famous statue of Lady Justice. She is holding the scales of justice, representing impartiality and the obligation of the law (through its representatives) to weigh the evidence presented to the court.

She is wearing a blindfold, representing the impartiality and objectivity of the law and that it doesn't let outside factors, such as politics, wealth or fame, influence its decisions.

She is bearing a sword, which symbolizes enforcement and respect, and means that justice stands by its decision and ruling, and is able to act. The fact that the sword is unsheathed and very visible is a sign that justice is transparent and is not an implement of fear. A double-edged blade signifies that justice can rule against either of the parties once the evidence has been perused, and it is bound to enforce the ruling as well as protect or defend the innocent party.

She is not cowering behind some edifice with eyes cast on how her actions might lead to violence. She is the upholder of the rule of law, not to mob rule.

This man in Cincinnati tried to take the law into his own hands and paid the ultimate price. Those who threaten violence if Trump is indicted will no doubt face the full force of the nation's criminal justice system, just as those January 6 rioters have learned.

It is worthy to note what some learned and respected leaders have said about our judicial system: "Our government... teaches the whole people by its example. If the government becomes the lawbreaker, it breeds contempt for law; it invites every man to become a law unto himself; it invites anarchy.".Justice Louis D. Brandeis

"No man is above the law, and no man is below it." Theodore Roosevelt

"We must remember that a strong and efficient criminal justice system is a guarantee to the rule of law and vibrant civil society." Justice R. M. Lodha

There is no other way for our criminal justice system to survive.

SENATOR LINDSEY GRAHAM'S THREAT OF VIOLENCE SHOWS HE DOESN'T CARE ABOUT THE RULE OF LAW.

Sen. Lindsey Graham warns that there will be violence in the streets if Donald Trump is charged with mishandling classified information.

Graham says there is a double standard of justice in not charging Hillary Clinton in connection with her mishandling of classified information on her private email server.

His effort to treat Trump as the functional or moral equivalent of Clinton is bogus. First, the Republican Party controlled both Congress and the White House from 2017 to 2019. If the Department of Justice and the FBI thought there was the slightest chance of a prosecution being successful, there is no doubt they would have charged her with anything, and try to make something stick. They didn't because even they knew they didn't have a case. Second, she didn't take any government records from her office a move them to her private, less secure residence. Third, she wasn't president of the United States with unique access to the most sensitive, top-secret records. Graham conveniently ignores the government's document classification system.

He also noted Hunter Biden, saying his father wouldn't have been elected president if his son had been charged. (At least Graham admits that Biden was elected.) Of course, speculation plays well into the hands of speculators. The fact is Hunter Biden is still under investigation by the prosecutor Trump chose before he left office. Moreover, trying to equate a private citizen's financial situation with those possible—and far more serious—crimes of a former president is what is known in logic as a false equivalence; there is simply no comparison.

But none of this matters to Lindsey Graham. He has long been a Trump stooge, and if such a statement came from anyone else under normal circumstances, it would be roundly and universally condemned as needlessly fanning the flames of violence by threats.

But he is not just anybody, and the circumstances he's trying to create certainly isn't normal. Such a statement coming from a United States senator is an outrage. Despicable is too nice a word for his rhetoric. His statement is a threat that not only fans those flames of violence, but is dangerous in that it presumes violence is acceptable to protect Trump. To call this woefully beneath the dignity of the office of United States senator would be a gross understatement. What he's saying plays perfectly to the party's base; that's why he's saying it.

This statement, coming from a leading figure of the political party that claims a monopoly on the rule of law, makes a mockery of that claim; further, it makes a joke out of being the party of law and order, and is the height of hypocrisy.

But, again, this doesn't matter to Lindsey Graham.

He says he's worried about the country. If that were true, he wouldn't be talking about a quid pro quo—the certainty of violence if Trump is criminally charged. He would be trying to calm the waters rather than throw oil on the fire.

His message is clear: it is a threat to the Biden Administration, to the Department of Justice, the FBI, and the United States attorney's office that would be in charge of any prosecution. It's the classic If-Then threat: if Trump is prosecuted, then the streets will be filled with violence.

Graham is right on one count; it is a matter of two systems of justice. But it isn't one for Clinton and the other for Trump. It's one for Donald Trump, the other for the rest of us.

It is perfectly proper under our justice system to gather evidence, match the evidence with the law, and if there is sufficient evidence to charge with a criminal violation, it is then a matter for the courts to assure that the defendant is accorded all of the rights found in our Constitution and constitutional jurisprudence.

Except for Donald Trump. For him, according to Graham, it doesn't matter what the evidence shows or even how much evidence there is. If he is charged, there will be violence. He alone is above the law and must never be held accountable or responsible for his actions. Graham also said that if there is violence, it will be law enforcement's fault.

This, from the party that prides itself on accountability and individual responsibility. This, from the party that champions law and order and claims to vigorously support law enforcement.

Only the deniers fail to see the blatant hypocrisy here.

Graham's purpose is to inject fear into our criminal justice system as applied to Trump. But fear can't and won't be a factor; Graham should be smart enough to realize that. Democracy can't survive on fear. The rule of law can't be suspended based on fear. The message sent to all Americans would be that prosecution can be avoided if defendants threaten violent reprisals. What this would do to our national security and safety should be self-evident.

What does Graham think will happen should Trump be charged? Does he think people like those on January 6 will storm the Department of Justice? The FBI headquarters? The courthouse that houses the United States attorney's office?

Law enforcement wasn't prepared for January 6. You can bet the mortgage that law enforcement is prepared now.

The question thus becomes what price are those who would engage in violence willing to pay for Trump? Are they willing to risk life and limb for him? Note that he hasn't provided legal counsel for those January 6 rioters now sitting in jail or awaiting trial. And he hasn't offered help to those yet to be charged and tried.

Recall that five died in the capital attack, and several law enforcement officers committed suicide since then. That loss of life hasn't moved Trump to help their families.

Instead of calling for calm and urging Trump's—and his—supporters to let our tried-and-true criminal justice system proceed as it has since the founding of our nation, we have this poor excuse for a high-ranking public official stoking violence.

Of course, he won't be at the front of any mob leading the charge; he'll be home where he will be safe and secure--like Trump was in the White House when all hell broke loose last year.

At least, Graham's that smart.

TRUMP'S LAWYERS ARE ON A LEGAL FISHING EXPEDITION TRYING TO AVOID THE CONSEQUENCES OF TAKING CLASSIFIED RECORDS TO HIS HOME.

A May 25 letter from one of Trump's lawyers, attached as an exhibit to the search affidavit, advances a broad view of presidential power, asserting that (1) the commander-in-chief has absolute authority to declassify whatever he wants, and (2) the "primary" law governing the handling of classified information simply doesn't apply to the president himself. The letter also implies that (3) these powers apply even after the president leaves office and is a private citizen again.

I suspect that the federal judge presiding over the Mar-a-Lago search warrant case—a Trump appointee—will find this too much of a stretch. She may set up the case to eventually reach the Supreme Court, which is most likely what Trump wants. At the very least, he hopes to delay the proceeding, figuring delay works to his advantage.

As you will soon see, Trump's problems with these three arguments is with the judiciary he helped create.

A liberal judge or justice might find that a former president has certain rights that are not specifically spelled out in the Constitution. You might recall Justice William O. Douglas's famous (or infamous) statement about the right of privacy in the famous (or, again, infamous) case involving contraceptives. (This is one case that Justice Clarence Thomas is urging the Court to re-visit.)

In Griswold v. Connecticut, Douglas said "Specific guarantees ….. have penumbras [fringe areas] formed by emanations from those guarantees that help give them life and substance." According to Douglas, "zones of privacy" emanate from the First Amendment's "penumbra" right of association, the Third Amendment's prohibition against the quartering of soldiers "in any house" without consent in peacetime, the fourth's guarantee against "unreasonable searches and seizures," and the fifth's privilege against self-incrimination.

Predictably, conservative jurists railed against this reading of rights into the Constitution they say are simply not there. It is this broad reading that led to the abortion rights decision of Roe v. Wade in 1973, which the Court overruled a few months ago.

Conservative jurists proudly claim to be originalists or textualists. Originalists search for the Constitution's original intent or original meaning; that is, they believe the Constitution must be interpreted based on what its drafters originally intended when they wrote it; textualists ask themselves what the words and phrases meant when a particular constitutional provision was adopted. Both textualists and originalists contend that the Constitution has permanent, static meaning; it can't be altered except by amendment.

Conservative judicial candidates promise to interpret the Constitution and laws as written, verbally slapping at the misguided "living Constitutionalists" like Justice Douglas.

But here's the rub. Article II of the Constitution sets out the executive powers of the president. There is nothing in that article that discusses declassifying information. The president's power to declassify flows from a Supreme Court decision, legislation passed by Congress, and executive orders. At least, so far.

It is a given that a president can declassify; how this is accomplished, however, is where Trump's lawyers are going. Although there is a statutory scheme for declassifying, Trump is arguing a president can simply declare it and it's done; a waving of the hand and it's a fait accompli.

A liberal jurist might buy this broad approach to constitutional interpretation, echoing that there are certain "penumbras" in Article II formed by "emanations" that give "life and substance" to presidential power. A conservative judge, however, will search in vain for any text that allows for a" waving of the hand" method of declassification, or for any intent by the framers to allow for this unchecked, cavalier approach to handling highly sensitive documents.

Trump's second argument—that the law doesn't apply to the president himself—is even more tenuous, at least for conservative jurists because, again, there is no language in the Constitution itself that sets up the president with blanket immunity from the nation's laws. These originalists/

textualists would have to find this language specifically set out in the Constitution, or find that it was the intent of the framers of Art. III to immunize the president from laws passed by Congress.

Considering that our nation was founded on the tyranny of the king of England, I doubt the framers intended to create an imperial presidency immune from the laws passed by Congress.

Finally, Trump's third argument is the greatest outreach: that these powers apply even after a president leaves office. Again, nothing in the Constitution even suggests that a former president has any power once out of office. He becomes a private citizen like us. Imagine conservative jurists trying to find language in the Constitution that deals with former presidents, or discerning the intent of the framers to grant powers and rights to former presidents. They ain't there.

TO THOSE WHO RELY ON THE "WHATABOUTISM" DEFENSE TO TRUMP'S BEHAVIOR, YOU NEED TO DO BETTER THAN THAT.

(Note: When folks take my posts to task by offering their contrary opinions, I typically respond by pointing out facts that refute the opinions, or I ask them for facts supporting their opinions. This typically ends the exchange. But after seeing numerous posts trying to refute mine by relying

on "whataboutism" in defense of Donald Trump, I had enough, and let this one poster know precisely how silly and meaningless this so-called defense is.)

Ah yes, the old "whataboutism" defense. Many of you rely on it because you think that justifies the behavior of your "stable genius." Here are some facts, which you obviously can't stand because they upset your uninformed opinions. For two years, from 2017-2019, the Republicans controlled both Congress and the White House, including the Department of Justice. Yet not a single charge was ever brought against Clinton. Do you know why? Because even they realized they didn't have a case against her that would stand up in court.

But since you want to play this silly "whataboutism" game, then what about Trump's rigged election lie, which cost five lives on January 6 and caused several law enforcement officers to commit suicide?

What about Trump stealing government records and taking them to his unsecured residence where they could be seen by others? Do you know whether Trump sold those records to anyone; perhaps a foreign government? You do know he's good buddies with Vladimir Putin and the North Korean dictator.

And let's take your "whataboutism" another step. What about Sen. Josh Hawley, who was seen cheering on the rioters? How about Reps. Marjorie Taylor Greene, Lauren Boebert, Jim Jordan, and so many others who continue to give Trump aid and comfort, hoping the American public will be distracted from Trump's behavior by buying into the "whataboutism" game.

You are entitled to your opinions, however warped and devoid of facts as they are. Adults are able back up their opinions with facts. Those you have attacked in your posts are waiting for your facts. We've had enough of your wild, factually unfounded opinions. We like to engage in intellectual discussions. That's impossible with you "whataboutism" folks right now. We hope you see fit to change by opening your eyes, stop defending the indefensible and cut out this "whataboutism" nonsense.

If you persist on relying on it, it only proves you have nothing else to offer.

NOW, ABOUT THOSE POLLS….

During Joe Biden's 18 months as president, he has been vilified by the Republicans for just about everything he's tried to do policy wise. A few months ago, his approval ratings were in the mid-30s.

At the end of August, however, his approval is now at 45%. This is what a couple of legislative victories will do to public sentiment.

Presidential polls are no different from any other poll; they represent a snapshot of public sentiment at the time the poll is taken. Reputable organizations such as Gallup, Quinnipiac and Marist conduct periodic polls of likely voters to gauge voting behavior at the moment. Nothing more, nothing less. They are extremely fluid, just like voters who change their minds as the wind blows.

You've heard the expression relating to polls "If the election were held today…" Well, the election is never being held when the poll is taken. But it is a contemporaneous measurement of present attitudes; this is the extent of its value and why people are generally interested in them, although that interest will vary from person to person.

Harry Truman was vilified by the Republican Party on a host of issues. At one point in his presidency, his approval rating was at 22%--lower than any president in American history. During various times in his nearly eight years in the White House, his approval ratings were in the 30s.

In 2021, a group of respected historians ranked Truman as the sixth greatest president in our nation's history, behind only Lincoln, Washington, FDR, Teddy Roosevelt and Eisenhower and ahead of Jefferson, Kennedy, Reagan and Obama. For methodology, 142 university historians and authors used a 1 ("not effective") to 10 ("very effective") scale to rate each president on 10 qualities of presidential leadership: "Public Persuasion, Crisis Leadership, Economic Management, Moral Authority, International Relations, Administrative Skills, Relations with Congress, Vision/Setting an Agenda, Pursued Equal Justice for All and Performance Within the Context of the Times." This resulted in the ranking of all presidents. (Biden was not included because of his very short tenure at the time this survey was conducted.)

So much for the historical significance of polls as they relate to presidential performance.

During his term in office, Trump's approval ratings ranged from a high of 47% to a low of 37%.

He is ranked among presidents as tied for third lowest, just above Andrew Johnson and James Buchanan. These rankings were made before the Congressional hearings on January 6 and his taking of classified government records and storing them at his unsecured Mar-a-Lago resort. If any of this pans out in the form of criminal charges, you can expect Trump to drop to the bottom. As bad as Johnson and Buchanan were, they were never charged with a violation of criminal law.

I don't know whether there has ever been a book written that deals exclusively with the relationship (if any) between a president's poll numbers and his ranking among his fellow presidents. If not, it seems as if it would be an interesting study.

Presidents typically say they don't set policy or make decisions based on polls. Claiming to be above the fray makes for good politics, but whether this is true or not makes for solid speculation. For me, it's stretch of the imagination to believe that a politician who has attained the highest office the land would be oblivious to his popularity among the voters.

In any event, for those who place at least some value on polls, these numbers speak for themselves. For those who favor one party's poll numbers and reject the other side's, enjoy the numbers for your side. For those who don't place any value on polls, nothing here will matter.

BIDEN TAKES IT TO THE "MAGA" CROWD, WHILE TRUMP GOES OFF THE RAILS.

Following calls by the Republican Party's right-wing extremists to "Defund the FBI," President Joe Biden took the "MAGA" crowd to task.

Meanwhile, the head of the "MAGA" crowd went off the rails, demanding either a new election or his reinstatement as president, neither of which can nor will happen.

Recall it was these extremists who vigorously attacked as un-American the "Defund the police" chanters after police officers shot and killed unarmed men who posed no visible threat to life and limb. These same people are now demanding the FBI be defunded for daring to execute a lawfully issued search warrant to recover classified documents from Trump's home and resort, documents that were unlawfully taken from the White House. By law, those records belong to the government, not Donald Trump.

Defunding the FBI is equally un-American, but that doesn't seem to bother them.

Biden laid it on the line to the MAGA crowd: "It's sickening to see the new attacks on the FBI, threatening the life of law enforcement and their families, for simply carrying out the law and doing their job. I'm opposed to defunding the police; I'm also opposed to defunding the FBI."

He also laced into GOP officials who still refuse to denounce the pro-Trump rioters who breached the U.S. Capitol nearly 20 months ago. Referencing Trump's "Make America Great Again" slogan, Biden said, "Let me say this to my MAGA Republican friends in Congress: Don't tell me you support the law enforcement if you won't condemn what happened on the 6th." Five died in that assault, and several law enforcement officers committed suicide.

Biden finally and vigorously voiced what Democrats have been saying—and many Republican have been feeling--for some time now. The difference is that Republicans remain fearful of Trump's influence on the party's base, and its effect on the upcoming elections.

He also called out Sen. Lindsey Graham for his inflammatory statement about "violence in the streets" if Trump is indicted. "The idea you turn on a television and see senior senators and congressmen saying, 'If such and such happens there'll be blood on the street'?" Biden said. "Where the hell are we?" During a political rally in the

Washington suburbs, Biden likened Republican ideology to "semi-fascism."

The Republicans are understandably nervous as the midterm elections draw near. Just a few months ago, they were licking their chops over the size of their majority in Congress next year, threatening to impeach Biden and investigate all those who dared to vote to impeach Trump for multiple violations of law, as well as those who dared to question him.

Now, buoyed by significant legislative accomplishments and with Biden's approval rating at 45%, the Democrats are energized by a brighter political climate.

Biden well understands the importance of timing in politics. Thirty-six years in the Senate and eight as vice president taught him well:. don't act until the timing is right. Now, the timing is right. Of course, the few remaining moderate Republicans understand the importance of timing; but that's not who controls the party now.

As for Trump, his latest maddening rant is driven by news that Facebook temporarily limited a controversial story about Hunter Biden's laptop in news feeds before the 2020 election. The laptop story had several red flags that raised questions about its authenticity and CEO Mark Zuckerberg said Facebook limited its reach on the site's news feeds for five or seven days because of the article's legitimacy.

Trump writes on his Truth Social that "THE FBI BURIED THE HUNTER BIDEN LAPTOP STORY BEFORE THE ELECTION." He says he would have won had it come out, though that is more than debatable given that Joe Biden won seven million more votes. Of course, private citizen Hunter Biden wasn't running for president in 2020, unlike Hillary Clinton in 2016.

It goes without saying that neither an immediate election nor his immediate reinstatement is possible. Neither one is going to happen.

For the Republican leadership trying to regain a majority in Congress, facing an energized Democratic Party with Trump as baggage is both frustrating and disconcerting to them. Trump is simply a distraction from the party's focused goal.

So, what is Trump's purpose in injecting his woes into the party's plan? He is either trying to keep his dwindling base energized with anger or impossible hope, or he genuinely believes his latest round of nonsense despite being told repeatedly the election wasn't rigged and he can't legally stash government records in his home, and there is no legal authority for what he now seeks.

If he's trying to remain relevant as more and more Republicans distance themselves from him, it's a sad commentary on how he views the intelligence level of his base. He actually believes they will buy this lunacy whole hog. He hopes they will believe what he posts on what he laughingly calls his Truth Social, while ignoring everything else that clearly establishes who he is and what he represents. That's not a positive statement about the intellectual prowess of his loyalists.

If he truly believes what he's feeding his people, however, then he doesn't belong in the White House, or even Mar-a-Lago. He needs to be institutionalized because he has lost all touch with reality.

THOSE HORRIBLE DEMOCRATS!

Those horrible Democrats! It's all their fault.

Their vigorous attacks really started when they dared to challenge our beloved former (and real) President Donald Trump over his magnificent response to COVID. Can you imagine such folks like Dr. Anthony Fauci and Dr. Deborah Birx challenging the smartest president we've ever had! So what if they're doctors with many years of experience. So what if they've published articles and are considered by others as experts in their fields. Trump doesn't need a fancy degree or experience in dealing with these kinds of diseases. What Trump knows in his gut makes him smarter than all of these so-called experts.

And everybody knows Trump won the election. That includes the false president Joe Biden. Those more than 60 judges who couldn't or wouldn't see the truth agreed with those evil Democrats. Yeah, I know lots of those judges—including the ones he appointed to the Supreme Court—ruled against him, but they were really Democrats then. Fortunately, the eventually saw the light of day and became Republicans, and real true conservatives, too.

Fortunately, they switched just in time to get rid of that horrible right to abortion, their so-called right to choose. Imagine that: women making their own decisions about their own person. We can't allow that to happen. We know what's best for all women. Telling them what their choices must be in the real American way.

Whoo, I got a bit sidetracked here. Back to the election. Everybody knows that the January 6 attack on the capital was caused by the Democrats. They dressed up like Trump supporters and stormed our sacred national treasure, hoping to make Trump look bad. When he urged those people to go to the capital, he knew he was really talking to the never Trumpers, and that they would attack the capital chanting his name, which the media would quickly pick up. He did this because this would keep his name in the public eye and all the real Trump lovers solidly in his corner.

Well, it's either that or those folks were just a few overeager Trump supporters engaging in legitimate political discourse. You can take your pick on the riot thingy.

And about those classified records, everybody knows there's nothing secret about them. The FBI and the Justice Department have created a real show about nothing. We know Trump likes to brag a little bit, so since he probably showed at least some of those records to his friends and associates (I don't know about his buddies in Moscow or Pyongyang, which I think is the capital of North Korea), they can't be secret anymore, right? Like I say, it's a big nothingburger.

Everybody also knows that all this talk about violence is just another way to distract us from basking in the true glory of Donald J. Trump. He is truly and without question the greatest president in American history. If he would just be immediately installed as president, or perhaps after a quick election that could be held in a matter of days, all this talk of violence would stop. I know, the Democrats and their so-called constitutional experts say this can't happen. Well, we can't let an old piece of paper decide what's best for the country, now can we?

A large number of historians from universities across the country rank Trump third from the bottom of all presidents. What do these so-called experts really know? They're too busy writing books and articles, and studying American history to see the true value of Trump and his magnificent policies and programs that are making America great again.

His intellectual prowess, creativity and supreme intelligence are well-known to everyone. The most brilliant and intellectually powerful men and women in Congress uniformly attest to Trump's unique status among American leaders throughout history.

Just ask such heavyweights like Sens. Ted Cruz, Josh Hawley, Rand Paul, John Kennedy (not the former president), Tom

Cotton, Lindsey Graham, etc., and Reps. Kevin McCarthy, Jim Jordan, Marjorie Taylor Greene, Lauren Boebert, Matt Gaetz, Mo Brooks, Paul Gosar, etc. and Governors Greg Abbott, Ron DeSantis and Doug Ducey, etc.

Democrats like to accuse these supremely intelligent elected representatives of promoting conspiracy theories, favoring white nationalists, re-writing history, trashing academic freedom via thought control policing, enacting suppressive voting laws designed to cut into opposition voting, etc. Democrats say if they can make law that makes illegal legal, or makes legal illegal, they'll do it. Well, to this I say: picky, picky.

What a horrible thing to say about these conservative scholars. They are promoting traditional conservative values. So what if a couple of people dressed up as law enforcement officers died on January 6. So what if others like them committed suicide. So what if some conservatives ignored subpoenas and asked for pardons. We're still the party of law and order and the rule of law, and don't let anybody tell you differently.

Those horrible Democrats have even gone after Trump's most loyal governors, accusing them of banning books and removing classes from schools, colleges and universities that make our young students feel uncomfortable. Education should be a joyful experience. We don't want to clutter up their little minds with stuff that might upset them. After all, what you don't know can't hurt you, right?

The Democrats warn that if we don't teach so-called important stuff to our young, they won't learn those lessons that will allow them to avoid dangerous problems in the future. That notion about history repeating itself is nonsense. I mean, if you don't know something, how can you repeat it? You can't repeat what you don't know. How can Democrats be so stupid!!

Besides, we all know that telling people what to read and what they can't read; and what to study and what they can't study, is real freedom. Allowing people to make these decisions all by themselves is tyranny. Again, we know what's best, and that's making America great again!

Personally, I can't wait for the day that America is run by Trump and his loyal geniuses like those named above. Think of the wonderful policies and programs that will flow from such ingenuity! It will make those horrible presidents like Franklin Roosevelt and Harry Truman look like the evildoers they were, no matter what historians say.

To the Democrats who say we're trying to dumb down our education system and make society not so smart, I say: well, duh!! We know what's best for everyone.

As Donald Trump says every time he speaks the truth: "Believe me." And we do, without giving this a second thought. Or any thought, for that matter.

End of story.

IS THIS FLORIDA'S SUCCESS STORY?

The Republican Party has been in power in Florida since 1999. It gained steam during the two terms of Gov. Rick Scott, and really took off under Gov. Ron DeSantis.

To see how the Republican Party leadership has done, let us look at three serious and far-reaching issues over the past few years as quoted from various news sources: such areas as rising sea levels, homeowners insurance and students' civic literacy. Then, let's look at how the party leaders have handled them.

First, rising sea levels.

"Overall, sea level rise is making the odds of a South Florida flood reaching more than four feet above high tide by 2050 on par with the odds of losing at Russian roulette. More than half the population of more than 100 Florida towns and cities lives on land below that 4-foot line.

The world's seas have absorbed more than 90 percent of the heat from these greenhouse gases, but it's taking a toll on our oceans: 2021 set a new record for ocean heating. Increasing ocean acidification, sea level rise and the increase of red tide are alarming as they can directly harm Florida's marine ecosystems, fisheries, and tourism. Rising seas is one of those climate change effects."

Second, homeowners insurance.

"Florida's crumbling homeowners insurance market is exposing one of the state's long-running flaws: its reliance on a single company to certify the majority of the state's insurers.

For the last few weeks, state regulators and Gov. Ron DeSantis' administration have been scrambling to contain the fallout after the state's primary ratings agency, Ohio-based Demotech Inc., warned of downgrades to roughly two dozen insurance companies, according to the state.

The downgrades would have triggered a meltdown of the state's housing market, a pillar of Florida's $1.2 trillion economy. Without the ratings, a million Floridians could be left scrambling to seek new insurance policies, possibly triggering a housing crisis in the middle of hurricane season and months before the November election."

Third, civic literacy under Florida's education governor.

"The state has issued a new Florida Civic Literacy Examination to assess how well public-school students understand what's called 'civic literacy.'" Kids in a U.S. government course are required to take the new exam that covers everything from landmark Supreme Court cases to influential documents in American history to basic principles about how government functions.

But so far, the first-time results are low: Only 37 percent of students passed in the 2021-22 school year. Students can pass with at least 60 percent correct answers on the computer-based exam, which includes approximately 80 items."

These represent three of the most critical issues facing our state. What has the Republican Party been doing about them?

As to the rising seas levels brought about by climate change, well, the state's leaders are finally coming around, albeit slowly, to say, well, maybe there is such a thing as global warming and climate change brought about by greenhouse gases., fossil fuels, etc. But, then again, maybe not. We know what most scientists say, but there are some who aren't so sure. Let's wait and see what happens. Meanwhile, we'll use a few band aids lying around to see if they work.

As for the homeowners insurance industry, this potential collapse is born of the number of strong storms that have hit the state over the past few years; storms that are a direct result of climate change, according to reputable scientists. Experts say warming waters make the storms more powerful, resulting in more rain and higher winds, which in turn cause greater damage to homes, etc.

What are Florida's leaders doing to solve this problem? As the hurricane season goes into full gear making time of the essence, they are still "scrambling" for an answer.

Finally, what about the low scores in civics literacy. Perhaps DeSantis and his legislative followers believe cutting off areas of curriculum study and teaching to make kids feel good about themselves is a good thing. It certainly appeals to the conservative masses by eliminating those pesky, annoying classes that teach kids about life in the real world. But we can't have these youngsters gain too much education. Then, they'll ask uncomfortable questions, the most dangerous being "why?" And the current version of the party can't tolerate anyone questioning their cultural adjustments. Against the backdrop of these low scores, DeSantis is currently campaigning for re-election, claiming he's expanded civics education.

Historians say the Republican Party is great at arousing fear and anger; the Democrats are better in legislating and policymaking. The best example is right after the stock market crash of 1929, and the lead-up to World War II.

The Hoover Republicans wanted business to right itself, with the now-comedic slogans "We are turning the corner" and "A chicken for every pot." They didn't want government to interfere in the affairs of big business. The voters saw through this fog and elected Franklin Roosevelt, who with a now-Democratic Congress, enacted legislation to deal with the seriously damaged economy wrought by the Republican Party. We can only imagine how things might have turned out had the Republicans been in charge of managing the Great Depression.

In the lead-up to World War II, Republican isolationists fought against our assisting Great Britain even as Hitler was building a mighty war machine. The leading isolationist,

Charles Lindbergh, urged our government to appease Hitler. Roosevelt's hands were tied, until Japan attacked Pearl Harbor. The Republicans became eerily silent, but they didn't go away. They merely bided their time. And we are witnessing the results of their doggedness and determination today. Again, we can only imagine how things might have turned out had the Republicans been in charge of managing our war effort.

There was a lack of leadership then by the Republicans, and the three examples here hardly demonstrate real leadership in action today. Rather, it demonstrates leadership inaction. They're very good at that.

THE INSURRECTIONISTS AMONG US.

Yesterday, historian and author Heather Cox Richardson noted that former House Speaker and Trump supporter Newt Gingrich (among others) was behind the post-election plan to arouse anger and stoke violence. This is what he said: "The goal is to arouse the country's anger through new verifiable information the American people have never seen before[.]... If we inform the American people in a way they find convincing and it arouses their anger[,] they will then bring pressure on legislators and governors." Of course, there never was any such "verifiable information." He is also responsible for driving moderates out of the party

Richardson also notes that Ginni Thomas, wife of Supreme Court Justice Clarence Thomas, wrote to lawmakers in

Arizona and Wisconsin urging them to appoint their own electors rather than the ones Joe Biden won. Again, this was done without a shred of supporting evidence.

And once again, Donald Trump sides with the January 6 rioters, saying how poorly treated they've been, and promises to consider pardons for all of them should he regain the White House. With all of this fanning the flames of violence, as soon as Joe Biden called out the MAGA crowd for what it is, Trump's willing stooge and House Speaker wannabee, Kevin McCarthy blasted Biden for being partisan and that it is Biden that is dividing the country.

The MAGA gang's efforts to blame Biden is quickly seen as a feckless attempt to flip the switch on the violence instigators. But to the MAGA bunch, it follows precisely what Gingrich and others have been advocating for some time now: violence, unless the extreme right wing gets its way.

Recall that five people died in the capital riot; several law enforcement officers took their own lives. We know that 147 right-wing House members voted to challenge the 2020 election results, once again without a shred of supporting evidence. Sen. Lindsey Graham threatens violence if Trump is prosecuted for stealing government records, yet does nothing to quell this threat.

It is now abundantly clear what the MAGA-run Republican Party means by the rule of law: arousing anger, making violence acceptable, pardoning lawbreakers, refusing to accept the results of an election that the evidence showed in every court was conducted fairly and freely, and on and on. And we now know, equally sadly, what the party means by personal responsibility and accountability--this doesn't apply to Trump or his MAGA gang. They are either fooling themselves, or they find democracy abhorrent and seek to install an authoritarian form of government.

TRAGEDY IN JACKSON, MISSISSIPPI.

Before the finger-pointing and blame game begin, with Mississippi officials blaming the Biden Administration for an inept FEMA response, it's important to recognize that the flooding and drinking water humanitarian crisis beleaguering Jackson, Mississippi didn't happen suddenly.

The tragedy now hitting the city is due in large part to long-neglected effects of climate change and infrastructure deterioration. Yet, when the problems born of this negligence rises, the states-righters who resent federal involvement in state affairs run to the federal government for help.

At least Biden was able to negotiate legislation that addresses both problems, although not as forcefully as necessary. The Republicans don't want to overburden their big business partners---the ones who give huge amounts of money in return for favorable tax and business legislation.

It is worth remembering that when you point the finger at someone, you have three fingers pointing at you.

MY RESPONSE TO A KNEE-JERK DEFENSE OF THE MAGA REPUBLICANS

(An old friend took to task one of my Facebook posts that quoted Harry Truman as saying about the Republican Party: "I never did give anybody hell. I just told the truth, and they thought it was hell." I broke down his rant into nine points. Here are his points, and my refutation of each one.)

1. "accuse the sitting president of being a Russian spy."

Facts. Our intelligence agencies uncovering information that Trump had help from the Russians in the 2016 campaign. This has never been refuted. In fact, the Senate Intelligence Committee in 2020 that Trump did have Russian assistance in 2016. And the Senate was controlled by Republicans in 2020.

2. "impeach him for something, anything"

Facts: Trump was impeached for asking the president of Ukraine dirt on Hunter Biden he could use in his re-election campaign in return for release of congressionally appropriated funds. This is a clear violation of federal law.

After Trump's pathetic display in Helsinki when he fawned over Putin's denial of Russian involvement in the 2016 election, accepting his word over the unanimous view of our intelligence agencies. This, from a man who covets strength and abhors weakness. No president ever appeared as weak or condescending to a Russian leader in our nation's history. Can you imagine Ronald Reagan bowing before a Russian leader, just short of kissing his ring? Well, perhaps you can.

3. "weaponize federal agencies and use them to investigate Hillary, Nancy and Hunter".

Facts: From 2017 to 2019, both Congress and the White House were controlled by Republicans. They also ran the Justice Department. Yet, not a single charge was ever filed against Clinton. Even Trump's own DOJ concluded that they didn't have a case against her that would stand up in court.

As for Hunter Biden, he is currently under investigation by the Justice Department; the investigation is headed by a Trump appointee.

I don't what crimes Nancy Pelosi is supposed to have committed; perhaps you would share your information with the local United States attorney.

And if you're really concerned about weaponization of federal agencies, you do remember Trump demanding personal loyalty from FBI Director James Comey. But perhaps you might find attempts to compromise the FBI direction a "perfect" demand, just like Trump's call to the

Ukraine president was a "perfect" call. Only it is against the law.

4."Find a politically sympathetic federal judge and find some reason to search the Biden residences and get the new AG to explain the justification for it.

Facts: Trump's residence was the subject of a lawfully issued probable cause subpoena because he stole government records from the White House and secreted them in his home and elsewhere around his property. Trump and his lawyers were asked several months ago if all records had been turned over to the government. After it was learned that they falsely said they were, the warrant was sought and executed. if you have evidence, other than creature of your creative mind, to prove the contrary, or that the judge was biased, I'm sure the U.S. attorney would be happy to receive it.

We are now learning just how careless Trump has been with those records, mixing highly classified documents in with his newspaper clippings, clothing and other personal belongings. Who knows who might have seen those records on nuclear weapons and other top-secret information. This is malfeasance, in addition to clear violations of federal law. But I guess that doesn't bother you.

5. "demand Biden and Harris full disclosure of tax returns for the last 20 years, subpoena all of their tax records and leak private investment matters",

Biden has made full disclosure of his tax returns, as every president before him has done, except Trump. The 20-year demand stems from his shady business dealings over many years. Harris, too, has disclosed her tax returns. Trump's returns were secret, until a news source broke the story and some of his tax returns were made public. He has yet to deny what those news report contained, except calling all things negative about him a "hoax."

6. "refuse to release health records and criminal history of the President and key administration personnel."

Facts: Biden has released his health records through his treating physician of many years. I don't know why you added criminal history; if you have information about the criminal history of Biden, Harris or anyone in his administration, please take it to the U.S.. attorney's office here. The criminal investigative authorities certainly have their hands full investigating the many potential criminal laws it clearly appears Trump has broken.

7. They might even investigate the riot and forced entry into the Dept of Interior building that resulted in dozens of arrests and injuries, including federal security officers and charge and imprison many native Americans who were involved.

Facts: the only riot that has been reported is the one Trump instigated by his inflammatory rhetoric on January 6, 2021. That riot was based on Trump's rigged election lie—a lie he perpetuates to this day. Contrary to the RNC, this was not just some pro-Trump supporters engaging in legitimate political discourse. Now, MAGA leaders are threatening violence if Trump is held accountable for his actions. If this is your party's definition of law and order, or the rule of law, then it is a warped view. Further, the party of personal responsibility and individual accountability evidently means only as applied to everyone else, and not to Trump, his loyalists in Congress, or his MAGA gang. Trump now promises to pardon those currently in prison or awaiting trial, if they, too, are imprisoned. Law and order! Rule of law! Ben, I have to believe you're better than this.

8."The new congressional leaders could even find a street thug and make him a national hero",

It seems the Republican leaders in 2016 might well have found that person, yet still want to make him a national hero.

You really surprise me with your shoot-from-the-hip comments. Nowhere do you even mention the laws Trump violated that led to two impeachments, or the laws implicated by his purloining of government records and carelessly strewing them around Mar-a-Lago.

You make no mention of the 147 House members who objected to the election results without a shred of evidence.

You make no mention of Kevin McCarthy's and Jim Jordan's promise to impeach Biden, for "something, anything," as you so eloquently put it.

Democrats could well make a claim that the federal judge overseeing Trump's classified documents, a Trump appointee, is politically sympathetic to him. But that would be childish and beneath the dignity of anyone even suggesting it. And besides, it was several of Trump's own judicial appointees who rejected his bogus rigged election claims.

Quite frankly, I'm getting tired of having to point-by-point refute the stuff you post. You are, of course, entitled to your opinions; you are not entitled to your facts.

If you have something of fact to inform law enforcement or prosecutorial agencies, then please do so.

I don't expect anything here will change your mind. You are so focused on defending the indefensible, you fail to see the forest through the trees.

I enjoy having a philosophical discussion with you, but this isn't philosophy. And it's certainly not political or policy differences. What the MAGA wing of the Republican Party represents is precisely what Joe Biden said last night.

But you won't agree with me, and I sure as hell will never agree with you.

"I DID NOTHING WRONG."

Every time Donald Trump is accused of a wrongdoing, or is seen with his hand in the cookie jar, his reaction is along the line of "I did nothing wrong."

After the August 8 search of Trump's Mar-a-Lago home and resort, he ranted about how he was invaded by FBI agents on a search and grab mission. At that time, he said "I did nothing wrong."

In news stories today, and in Heather Cox Richardson's column, the implications of Trump's secretive actions are becoming more and more startling. The unsealing of a Department of Justice court filing revealed that the search turned up more than 11,000 documents or photographs that were not classified, 31 documents marked CONFIDENTIAL, 54 marked SECRET, and 18 marked TOP SECRET. In addition, agents found 48 empty folders marked CLASSIFIED, and 42 empty folders marked to be returned to a military aide. Those documents were not filed with the envelopes.

As author and historian Richardson notes: "This story is unprecedented and explosive. As Sue Gordon, who was principal deputy director of national intelligence from 2017 to 2019, told MSNBC's Nicolle Wallace yesterday, in addition to the potential for exposing national secrets, the exposure of the networks and techniques that were in those documents could unravel intelligence networks that took decades to build.

The implications for the destruction of our national security at Trump's hands are enormous."

Yet, Trump persists that he "did nothing wrong."

When he rejected the unanimous findings by our intelligence agencies that Russia helped Trump in the 2016 election, he chose to believe Russian dictator Vladimir Putin's bare denial in that infamous meeting in Helsinki in 2017. There, Trump all but bowed down to Putin, showing extreme weakness at a time when strength and confidence in our national security system were absolutely necessary. A 2020 Senate Intelligence Committee backed the findings and conclusions of our intelligence agencies.

"I did nothing wrong."

His apathetic response to the COVID outbreak, where he even suggested injecting bleach to kill the virus, might have caused sickness and death to an untold number of people.

"I did nothing wrong."

He placed an illegal "perfect" call to the president of Ukraine seeking dirt on Joe Biden's son during the 2020 campaign in return for releasing funds approved by Congress.

"I did nothing wrong."

He knowingly lied about the 2020 election results, despite every court's rejection of his unsupported claims.

"I did nothing wrong."

He instigated a mob of loyal supporters to attack the capital on January 6, 2021, resulting in five deaths and subsequent suicides by law enforcement personnel.

"I did nothing wrong."

Buying into a clearly illegal scheme, he demanded that this vice president unconstitutionally reject the Electoral College results, thereby forcing the election into the Republican controlled House of Representatives.

"I did nothing wrong."

Sadly, in this latest in a series of episodes, purloining highly classified government records from a public building—the White House—and secreting them in his unsecured resort, he responds with his now all-to-familiar plaintiff bleat, a wavering wail of a goat or sheep:

"I did nothing wrong."

To someone with no moral compass, or the ability to distinguish right from wrong, the cry of "I did nothing wrong" is not surprising. Narcissists and egomaniacs never do anything wrong. They are perfect in every way. They are pathological liars to everyone except themselves and their blind and deaf loyalists. They are legends in their own mind. Remember Trump referred to himself as a "stable genius." Remember his famous line: "I alone can fix it."

Now we know how well he has fixed things. Look at the number of people who've risked their own lives for him. Look at how many are now wallowing in jail—with more to come—for believing his lies; for believing in him. Look at how many sent him money—and are still sending him money—by accompanying his attacks on those trying to hold him accountable with a plea for cash.

He is the consummate snake oil salesman, and as P. T. Barnum said, "There's a sucker born every minute."

While in office, he disparaged our allies, dissed NATO, and empowered Putin and North Korea's Kim Jong-il. He repeatedly bashed our intelligence agencies—evidently he knew things we didn't know back then—dissed his military advisors when they offered advice he didn't like, saying he was smarter than them, and did whatever he could to undermine our Democracy.

And we are paying dearly for his devious behavior.

There is little doubt that at least some of Trump's congressional loyalists are staying with him because of his influence on the base, the MAGA minions. But once that base begins to implode, perhaps those loyalists, seeing that their re-election to office doesn't depend on them, will do what others like Bill Barr and Trump's former military advisors are doing--abandoning him and his madness. Hope springs eternal.

In passing, what is sad is that there are several who owe Trump nothing; folks like Mitch McConnell and Lindsey Graham would have won without him, and they will be in the Senate long after Trump is history. Why they stick with Trump, either begrudgingly or vigorously, will be a source for study by future historians.

Justice, however, has a way of seeing through the fog Trump has wrapped around the Republican Party. Already, more and more of his one-time loyalists are breaking rank, saying in effect "enough is enough."

Sadly, there will no doubt be more stark revelations ahead. The FBI's analysis of the seized records is not complete, and then there are those House hearings on the January 6 attack that will be televised right up to the midterm elections. The damning evidence of Trump's illegal behavior is coming from Republicans, though not the kind that have taken over a once proud political party.

Hopefully, more and more will wake up from the nightmare of Trumpism over the next couple of months.

Years from now, historians will have a veritable field day dissecting the Trump presidency and its existential threat to Democracy.

But as the walls continue to close in on him; as more and more deflect from Trumpism; and as the cell doors (in his mind and, perhaps literally) close, we will no doubt hear once again—perhaps for the final time--his braying, plaintiff wail echoing in the wind; the final whimper of the lad caught with his hand in the cookie jar:

"I did nothing wrong."

Only then, it won't matter.

REPUBLICANS NEVER PLAY PARTISAN POLITICS. ANOTHER MYTH FROM THE RIGHT.

Republicans are constantly accusing Democrats of playing partisan politics. But, of course, Republicans would never do a thing like that. Right! Here's a classic example of Republicans not playing politics. It's just a coincidence that 20 felons were investigated and charged with voter fraud by Florida Gov. Ron DeSantis's election police force just days before the primary elections. And it's just happenstance that the announcement was made in Democrat-leaning counties. Never mind the timing; it's all about voter fraud which by the way has not been found to exist in Florida.

After the 2020 election, he said it was a smooth, error-free election. Guess he and his cronies forgot about that. Anyway, to prove a criminal case, the state elections police force will have to prove these 20 intentionally and willfully cast a vote. This means the state will have to prove that when they voted, they knew they couldn't and voted anyway. Good luck with that, Ron.

But that really doesn't matter. It made for good press and excited his supporters. It plays well to the MAGA gang. Besides, by the time these 20 are released from their charges, it will most likely be after the November elections. And if the charges are dropped before then, Ron could simply blame the liberal courts. It's a win-win for him--if you don't mind being played.

MY RESPONSE TO "THROW ALL THE RASCALS OUT" CLAIM.

I would certainly agree with you if the problems were relatively similar. But whatever the Democrats have done, they don't compare to what we've been seeing from the Republicans over the past few years. This isn't about policy differences; it's about attacks on our nation's historic choice of the type of government we want.

Certainly, the Democrats never lied about presidential elections, knew that they lied about it, and instigated a crowd to attack our nation's capital. No Democrat president ever told his VP to reject the Electoral College vote. No Democrat president ever stole government records and stored them in his home in unsecured areas, and then said he did nothing wrong.

I could go on and on about what Trump has done to undermine our government, like his rejection of the unanimous conclusion of our intelligence agencies that he had Russian help in 2016--believing Putin over his own government. A Senate Intelligence Committee report in 2020 agreed with our agencies' assessment. Trump chose to believe Putin. There are certainly other examples. And with each one, his Republican cronies chose to go with Trump out of fear, rather than with our nation's legal standards.

In response, please don't rehash the typical Republican Party line of "whataboutism." What about Hillary? What about Hunter Biden? First, they don't compare to what Trump and his cronies have done. Neither was a president of the United States. Second, the Republicans had every opportunity to charge Clinton when the party controlled Congress and the White House from 2017-2019, but even Trump's Justice Department realized they didn't have a case against her. As for Biden, he is currently under investigation by a Trump-appointed federal prosecutor.

Just saying throw out all the rascals doesn't make it so. There needs to be a factual and legal basis that the voters buy in order to accomplish that. Every president in our nation's history has honored that. But one.

IS TRUMP BEING PLAYED BY BIDEN?

I came across a fascinating article today in the Atlantic. The author, David Frum, contends that Donald Trump, blistering over Joe Biden's provocative speech in Philadelphia the other day, used a rally that was supposed to be in support of Pennsylvania's Republican candidates for governor and senator as a forum for airing his grievances and, more importantly, going off unhinged at Biden, the FBI and others who dare to cross him.

This is exactly what Biden intended by his speech.

With the midterm elections just around the corner, the last thing the Republican Party leadership wants is any distraction from focusing on retaking the House and Senate.

These party insiders are well aware that Trump never received a majority vote in either election; he lost the House in 2018, his re-election bid in 2020, and the two Georgia senate seats in 2021 that gave the Democrats control of the senate.

The Republicans wanted this campaign to be about inflation, gas prices, crime, the border—anything other than Donald Trump. The party leadership has said—gently, so as not to anger him--they want Trump to hold off announcing his presidential ambitions until after the November election.

But being a shrewd politician, Biden well knew and agreed with what Hillary Clinton said in 2016: that Trump is a fool who can be baited with a tweet. If that's so, Biden figured, what would a full-throated speech do to set off Trump in full battle mode.

Biden, knowing Trump hasn't met a spotlight he didn't like, set out the bait, accusing Trump and his MAGA cronies of stoking violence and being a threat to Democracy.

Having goaded Trump, he predictably took the bait and proceeded to lambast Biden as an "enemy of the state" and roundly condemned the City of Philadelphia, Pennsylvania's largest city.

In a rambling rant, Trump went off in multiple directions. He trashed the FBI, attacking it, and the Department of Justice, as "vicious monsters." As Frum noted, "He complained about the FBI searching his closets for stolen government documents, inadvertently reminding everyone that the FBI had actually found stolen government documents in his closet—and in his bathroom too. He abused his party's leader in the U.S. Senate as someone who 'should be ashamed.' He claimed to have won the popular vote in the state of Pennsylvania, which, in fact, he lost by more than 80,000 votes."

The two candidates Trump was supposed to endorse instead read this headline in the local newspaper the next day: "Donald Trump Blasts Philadelphia, President Biden During Rally for Doug Mastriano, Dr. Oz in Wilkes-Barre."

This is what Trump said about Philadelphia: "I think Philadelphia was a great choice to make this speech of hatred and anger. [Biden's] speech was hatred and anger. Last year, the city set an all-time murder record with 560 homicides, and it's on track to shatter that record again in

2022. Numbers that nobody's ever seen other than in some other Democrat-run cities."

Of course, while castigating Philadelphia for its crime rate, he inadvertently reminded others about his own serious exposure to the nation's criminal justice system. Stealing and mishandling classified government records is a clear violation of federal law. Let's see how Trump tries to squeeze out of this. His declassification claim is falling flat; his claim of having done "nothing wrong," is ringing hollow.

Biden couldn't have written a better speech than Trump's own wild ramblings; it was exactly the reaction Biden's speech was designed to elicit.

As with all his previous rallies, Trump's message in Philadelphia was all about him. A vote for a Republican candidate is a vote for Trump. A Republican vote is an endorsement of everything that is Trump.

Frum notes that Trump still dominates the Republican Party. "He has extracted support even from would-be rivals like Florida Governor Ron DeSantis—rituals of submission within a party hierarchy that respects only acts of domination.

Republican congressional leaders desperately but hopelessly tried to avert the risk that this next election would become yet another national referendum on Trump's leadership. Despite Trump's lying and boasting, politicians who can count to 50 and 218—the respective numbers needed for a majority in the Senate and House—have to reckon with the real-world costs of Trump's defeats. But Biden understood their man's psychology too well.

Biden came to Philadelphia to deliver a wound to Trump's boundless yet fragile ego. Trump obliged with a monstrously self-involved meltdown 48 hours later. And now his party has nowhere to hide. Trump has overwritten his name on every Republican line of every ballot in 2022.

Biden dangled the bait. Trump took it—and put his whole party on the hook with him. Republican leaders are left with little choice but to pretend to like it."

Meanwhile, Biden and his supporters will no doubt do everything they can to keep Trump right where he is: as the face and, perhaps more importantly, the voice of the Republican Party.

In doing so, the Democrats may have finally found their voice.

DANGEROUS TIMES, FAIR QUESTION.

We are a deeply polarized, divided nation. The term "United States" rings hollow in some quarters, as Americans threaten Americans with violence unless "they" have their way. Both our people and our government are miles apart on the great issues of our time.

It is therefore sad but necessary to ask this burning question: who benefits the most from our current state of affairs? Who stands to gain the most out of a weakened, demoralized America? The answer should be obvious.

One man is in Moscow; the other in Beijing. Vladimir Putin and Xi Jinping.

The man in Moscow is chomping at the bit for a weakened NATO. In his mind, a deeply divided, ideologically torn United States with polarized factions at each other's throat would be too weak to fend off Russia's power grab. This would allow him to pick off one nearby country after another, adding to his collection of nations loyal to Moscow, and to him.

NATO, which draws most of its strength from the United States, wouldn't be in a position to stop him. He would also have the geographic and logistical advantage. For Putin, the Ukraine is just a start. Putin realizes that Ukraine is a tough challenge; he's hoping a more polarized America won't be able to provide it—or any other country he chooses—with the flow of money and weaponry down the road to stop his advances.

Recall that Donald Trump sought to weaken NATO. He cozied up to Putin, believing the Russian dictator was his friend. But Trump was being played; he was no match for a 16-year former intelligence officer who rose to the rank of lieutenant in the KGB. Pitting a master spy against an egocentric no-nothing was a perfect fit for Putin. Until the 2020 election.

But presumably as smart as Putin is, he is maintaining at least a semblance of a relationship with Trump, who's only too eager to have a friend anywhere. (This raises a question about those classified documents. We'll have to wait this one out.)

Meanwhile, over in Beijing, Xi is busy keeping his fellow countrymen in line, building an even stronger military and economic foundation for his 1.4 billion subjects. He has his eyes on Taiwan, and he's keeping close watch on his eccentric, uneasy ally in North Korea.

Think of prize fighters, football teams, etc., probing their opponents for weaknesses, waiting for the right time and place to strike.

Like two serpents, Putin and Xi are eyeing America carefully, probing for weak spots, waiting to see when the right time will come to strike.

The anger, rage, hatred, possible violence, are drawing us closer and closer to the precipice. When both major political parties talk about a "battle for the soul of America" from the far ends of the political spectrum, we have reached a tipping point. It seems there is no room for compromise; that's the greatest danger we face today.

Historians and political pundits tell us we are two elections away from the demise of our form of government; that the almost 250-year experiment in self-governance is a failure. Benjamin Franklin warned us of this when he said our founding fathers forged a Democracy "if you can keep it." That statement is facing its greatest test since the Civil War.

Conservatives accuse the left of wanting to bring socialism to America. Liberals accuse the right of pandering to authoritarianism/Fascism.

When has the left ever proposed a socialist government? Never. Oh, we've had, and still have, vestiges of socialist programs. If you know your history, you will recall those programs that helped take our nation from the brink of economic disaster almost 100 years ago. Others are found in the civil and social rights acts of the 1960s. And recently, the infrastructure and climate change legislation fit the mold of socialist type programs. All of these have one thing in common: they help a majority of Americans.

When has the right ever proposed an authoritarian Fascist-type government? Not in so many words, but by deeds. Just read the newspapers, magazine articles; listen to news reports from reputable journalists. It's right there for those who choose to see it.

As trust in our nation's institutions continues to decline, polls show almost half of Americans believe we are headed to a second civil war. Who benefits from such a horrible thought? Two men named above.

So, how do we step back from the cliff and avoid losing our status as the beacon of Democracy, strong and steady? How do we avoid the dire opinion of a sizeable number of Americans? What must we do to keep the promise spoken by John Kennedy is his inaugural address over 60 years ago? Recall his words: “Let every nation know, whether it wishes us well or ill, that we shall pay any price, bear any burden, meet any hardship, support any friend, oppose any foe to assure the survival and the success of liberty.”

First, we must look at the example Conservative President Ronald Reagan and Liberal House Speaker Tip O’Neill gave us. On policy, they argued vociferously, but at the end of the day, they got together, forged compromises over food and drink, and the American public was better off for it. It’s that common thread that we must seek out. It is the thread that holds our nation together.

To those who believe conservatives and liberals can’t work together, I give you an example from today’s news where, in Idaho, conservatives join liberals in what is described as a “quiet and polite” protest to protect their library from book-banners.

Considering today’s dynamics, compromise isn’t easy, can be painful but it can be accomplished; indeed, it must be the singular goal if we are to move forward. This means electing representatives who promise not to bash the other side, but to find common ground. That’s governing, not pandering for the sake of arousing anger and rage.

Second, we must strive to govern in the middle, where compromises are forged. What is good for all Americans must be the goal of all government policies.

We must also face the uncomfortable fact that extremism has always been with us. It was present in the 1930s and 1940s during the leadup to World War II; it was there in the 1950s during the "red scare," and it's with us today from the far left but even more so from the far right. The latter has become so severe that our intelligence agencies have said that our nation's greatest threat comes from domestic terrorism on the right.

The forces that allowed radical extremism to gain public support must be quelled and relegated to distant outlier status again.

Joe Biden is a breather from his predecessor, but he's at the end of his political career. Plus, he models himself after Franklin Roosevelt. What FDR did via legislation and executive orders was necessary to prevent the economic collapse of America.

Times are different now. We have a strong economy and strong military. But both are at risk by division and hatred.

Third, moderation is the key. We need Republicans more in the mold of Barry Goldwater, William F. Buckley, Jr., and Ronald Reagan. We need Democrats more in the mold of John Kennedy, Lyndon Johnson and Bill Clinton. These represent varying degrees of moderation in both parties.

And the moderates must be young enough to know what harm radical extremism can do to our nation. They must be smart enough to know what programs and policies are best for all Americans. They must be knowledgeable enough about American history to avoid repeating its harsh teachings.

The specifics of what needs to be done are above my pay grade. But I do know this: while we can learn, we can't go back to the 1920s, 1930s or 1950s.

And the status quo isn't an option.

FEDERAL JUDGE APPOINTS SPECIAL MASTER TO EXAMINE CLASSIFIED DOCUMENTS TAKEN FROM TRUMP'S HOME AND RESORT.

This is a sop to Trump. This gives him what he wants now, a special master and delay. It will be interesting to see who gets the job. The Federal Rules of Civil Procedure allows a federal court to appoint a special master, with the consent of the parties, to conduct proceedings and report to the court. It's the consent of the parties that will be the immediate focus. Trump's going to want a lawyer favorable to him. If the Department of Justice wants to make an issue out of this, it could recommend two Republicans: Robert Mueller and James Comey. You can bet Trump would go ballistic over either one.

Both sides will have to approve whoever is chosen. You can bet it won't be Rudy Giuliani, John Eastman or any other lawyer associated with Trump's failed attempt to challenge the 2020 election, or who continue to forge ahead with Trump's "rigged election" lie, or who otherwise believe Trump did nothing wrong either as president or since he left office.

Meanwhile, the FBI and Department of Justice are quite capable of reading tea leaves. With a Trump appointee judge, the prospect was always there that she would appoint a special master. Under the rules, she was under no mandate to do so. She could have had a federal magistrate do the review. That would have been much quicker than the time it will take to appoint a special master, have him get up to speed, and then go through the mass of documents the FBI has already examined.

And since the documents are quite voluminous, the question arises who else will be given the same authority as the special master.

So, while all this legal wrangling was going on, what would you expect the Department of Justice to do? Why go through every piece of paper they got, take pictures, make copies, etc. You can bet the mortgage that review of all relevant documents has been, or was just about to be, completed. So far, it looks like something that's full of sound and fury, yet signifies nothing.

All the Republican congressional leadership wants is to get to the November elections without Trump being a distraction. The judge's order allows intelligence officials to continue conducting a classification review, as well as a national security damage assessment review, so there will no doubt be more said on these fronts. Two things are important; first, who the special master will be, and how much time the judge will give him/her time to review and report.

Whatever decisions the special master makes, they will have to go through the vetting process to see what aren't government records; what are classified, perhaps the appropriate level of classification should be, what documents are covered by the attorney-client privilege, etc. And with each decision, there will undoubtedly be battles between Trump's lawyers and the DOJ. And then there's the appellate process to consider. Yes, there are interesting days--and months--ahead, leading to the "drip, drip, drip" toward 2024. Toss in the House committee's work leading to its final report later this year, and whatever DOJ does with the classified documents it's already reviewed, the march toward 2024 promises to be an unprecedented time in American history.

REPUTATIONAL HARM TO TRUMP. THAT'S A LAUGHER.

The federal judge overseeing the classified document review of records taken from Trump's home cites "reputational harm" to him as a basis for ordering the appointment of a special master.

We know the FBI found classified documents mixed with other items, including his tax and medical records, at Mar-a-Lago. Mishandling classified documents is a violation of law.

The FBI has already seen most, if not all, of what was removed. The agents could simply retain the classified documents referenced in the subpoena and return the rest to him.

Perhaps the judge bought the argument that Trump can't trust the FBI. If so, what makes the appointment of a special master any less suspect, especially if the appointed lawyer--most likely a retired judge--is someone Trump is suspicious of?

Presumably, the judge wants to retain complete control of the review process, to see that every record is examined and found to be covered by the subpoena; what records are protected by the attorney-client privilege; or protected by executive privilege (an potentially unprecedented review, since the question of whether a former president can claim executive privilege over documents created during his term, but is not claimed by the incumbent, has never been raised or addressed before); and which are personal records that can be returned to him.

But the obvious question from the judge's ruling is what harm to Trump's reputation could possibly come from the FBI's review of the records Trump took from the White House? His MAGA minions believe he walks on water; some believe he's mentally challenged with no moral compass; others believe he's a scourge on America. Even assuming the worst about him from those records, how would this change the opinions formed about him over the past six years?

And the beat goes on.

SOME OBSERVATIONS ABOUT THE FEDERAL JUDGE WHO RULED IN TRUMP'S FAVOR FOR A SPECIAL MASTER APPOINTMENT TO REVIEW WHAT THE FBI SEIZED FROM MAR-A-LAGO.

When the federal magistrate authorized the probable cause warrant leading to the search of Donald Trump's residence, his supporters blamed the FBI for selecting a judge favorable to the government's position on his taking of classified documents. They reasoned that only a hand-picked judge would have ruled that way. This shows ignorance of how judges are selected to preside over a case. Judges are chosen by lot. For example, each judge is given a letter of the alphabet. There's Judge A, Judge B...you get the point. If the prior case was assigned blindly to Judge A, the next case to be filed will be assigned to Judge B. There is no skipping, unless after the judge is assigned the case, a party points out some reason that judge should be recused, such as familiarity with the party, personal interest in the case, etc. There are rules that govern when a judge must recuse himself from a case. If a judge is recused, the case is then reassigned to the next available judge. Again by way of example, if Judge X is now the next judge, that's who will get the case.

But now that after the judge who is presiding over the Trump search and seizure case granted him his request for a special master, many are left wondering if this Trump-appointed judge was desirous of doing him a favor. Yesterday's column by Heather Cox Richardson makes this point quite vigorously. Here are a few excerpts from her column. Read the column in its entirety for the full impact of the judge's decision. Her column intimates that sometimes there is benefit in the luck of the draw.

"a Trump-appointed judge, confirmed by the Senate on November 13, 2020, after Trump had lost the election, has stepped between the Department of Justice and the former president in the investigation of classified documents stolen from the government.

Legal analysts appear to be appalled by the poor quality of the opinion. Former U.S. acting solicitor general Neal Katyal called it "so bad it's hard to know where to begin." Law professor Stephen Vladeck told Charlie Savage of the New York Times that it was 'an unprecedented intervention... into the middle of an ongoing federal criminal and national security investigation. 'Paul Rosenzweig, a prosecutor in the independent counsel investigation of Bill Clinton, told Savage it was 'a genuinely unprecedented decision' and said stopping the criminal investigation was 'simply untenable.' Duke University law professor Samuel Buell added: 'To any lawyer with serious federal criminal court experience…, this ruling is laughably bad…. Trump is getting something no one else ever gets in federal court, he's getting it for no good reason, and it will not in the slightest reduce the ongoing howls that he's being persecuted, when he is being privileged."

Energy and politics reporter David Roberts of Volts pointed out that this is a common pattern for MAGA Republicans. First, they spread lies and conspiracy theories, then they act based on the 'appearance' that something is shady. 'So this… judge says Trump deserves extraordinary, unprecedented latitude because of the 'extraordinary circumstances' and the 'swirling questions about bias.' But her fellow reactionaries were the only ones raising questions of bias! It's a perfectly sealed feedback loop," and one the right wing has perfected over "voter fraud.'"

"Something else jumps out about the judge's construction, though: it makes MAGA Republicans the only ones whose sentiments matter."

"The neutrality of the law is central to democracy. But it is increasingly under question as Republican-appointed judges make decisions that disregard settled law, and

Cannon's decision will not help. She actually singles out Trump as having a different relationship to the law than the rest of us in a number of ways, but especially when she expresses concern over how his reputation could be hurt by an indictment: 'As a function of Plaintiff's former position as President of the United States, the stigma associated with the subject seizure is in a league of its own. A future indictment, based to any degree on property that ought to be returned, would result in reputational harm of a decidedly different order of magnitude.'"

"Philosopher Jason Stanley of Yale University, best known for his 2018 book How Fascism Works, tweeted today: 'Once you have the courts you can pretty much do whatever you want.'"

"Cannon's decision addresses only the criminal investigation of the former president by the Department of Justice, and it is not clear how much of a delay it will create. While that is on hold, at least temporarily, the intelligence assessment by the Office of the Director of National Intelligence will proceed without check. It is still unclear what documents are missing, and who has had unauthorized access to the information Trump took.

This breach of our national security has the potential to be catastrophic."

EXPLAINING DONALD TRUMP'S POPULARITY AMONG HIS MLLIONS OF SUPPORTERS.

"I'm as mad as hell, and I'm not going to take this anymore!" This is the memorable line yelled by anchorman Howard Beale (played by Peter Finch) in the 1976 film "Network."

For years, the TV audience laughed at the antics of Jackie Gleason's Ralph Kramden, who complained to his long-suffering wife Alice of the indignities and struggles he endured as a bus driver, and just generally, living in New York.

Years later, the audience laughed at the outrageous bigotry and nonsense that came from Carroll O'Connor's Archie Bunker, who ranted to his long-suffering "dingbat" wife Edith about the daily indignities he suffered.

In each of these three made-for-entertainment incidences, the victim was Beale, Kramden and Bunker. The source of their anger, suffering, pain, insults, indignities, was "them.'" In each case, fiction wasn't far from fact.

Do you see the picture yet?

Over the years, since the wave of civil and social justice court decisions beginning with Brown v. Board of Education in 1954, to the legislation of the 1960s "Great Society" of Lyndon Johnson, anger, resentment, etc., have been slowly simmering beneath the surface in many parts of the country. Resentment over federal handouts to the undeserving; anger over the rise of the administrative state's deep intrusion into private lives; high costs and high taxes, etc.--the grievances kept piling up.

Although there certainly were conservative thinkers back then, most notably Sen. Barry Goldwater of Arizona and author William F. Buckley, Jr., they presented a policy-oriented counter to what they said was the unconscionable liberalization of government, leading to more centralized government, higher taxes, the rise of the welfare state, and the decline of individual responsibility.

Certainly, Ronald Reagan brought conservative thought to the forefront, but he infused it with magnanimity, working with House Speaker Tip O'Neill to forge compromises.

Compromise, however, was not what conservatives really wanted.

Then along came House Speaker Newt Gingrich and his 1994 wave of young conservatives eagerly supporting his contract for America. But he got caught up in a bit of a scandal which, following closely behind Bill Clinton's, didn't give this young group of eager, wide-eyed conservatives a chance to move their ideology along with Gingrich as its leader.

Besides, Clinton was a moderate Democrat who didn't create a wide ideological schism with the Republicans at the time. Back then, both parties had a significant number of moderates. Thus, government policy was controlled mostly by the center.

To many conservatives, however, the flashpoint was the election of Barack Obama in 2008. The resentment that had been slowly brewing over the years was now reaching full throttle. Obama was challenged at every opportunity by the rising conservative tide.

Into this mix stepped Donald Trump.

Imagine for a moment how a man of extreme privilege; one born and raised in liberal New York, became the voice of hard-working Joe Bucket; the voice of victims everywhere, reaching the minds, hearts and souls of the salesclerk in Dallas, the construction worker in Birmingham, the cashier in Biloxi, the stock clerk in Phoenix, and on and on.

He began telling his growing audience years ago that they were suffering the indignities of handouts to the undeserving, paid for by their tax dollars. He challenged Obama to produce his birth certificate—raising the unspoken undercurrent of racism. He made his audience all but shout "I'm mad as hell and I'm not going to take it anymore." He made his audience believe they were the victims of "them," much in the mold of Ralph Kramden. And he stoked outrage in the manner of an Archie Bunker.

He told his audience he felt their pain. And they believed him wholeheartedly. Trump made victimization popular.

It was, and remains, the greatest con game in American political history.

And it's continuing to pay off.

When he rants about how unfairly he's being treated, with all those investigation "hoaxes" that are targeting him, his audience identifies with his pain through theirs. It's a winning combination for him!

This is how he's been able to, in large part, campaign successfully for candidates who, by background, are woefully unqualified for public office. Dr. Mehmet Oz. Herschel Walker. Look at those he's helped elect to Congress. Marjorie Taylor Greene. Matt Gaetz. Lauren Boebert. He gave them and others their strident voices. Qualifications for office is not as important as ideological stance.

The point must also be made, however, that the Trumpites don't care about paper qualifications; what they do care about is having someone who speaks to their resentment, who arouses their ire, who makes them say "I'm mad as hell and I'm not going to take it anymore."

To drive home an obvious point, these election successes is not about policy; policymaking can be messy. There is a joke about the two things you never want to see made; sausage and legislation. Policymaking by legislation involves compromise; sometimes compromising on compromises. It can be nasty and time-consuming. Democrats have more policy wonks in the party's history than Republicans.

Recall that Franklin Roosevelt was a consummate policy wonk. So were Lyndon Johnson, Bill Clinton and Barack Obama. Joe Biden is no doubt a policy wonk as well, with 36 years in the senate and eight years as vice president mostly responsible for forging Obama's legislative plans.

Except for tax cuts primarily for the wealthy and a few other minor legislative proposals, Republicans haven't been as active policy wonks as Democrats. Recall that for several years, the Republicans promised to repeal Obamacare and replace it. That replacement legislation has never seen the light of day because there was never a plan to replace Obamacare.

Policymaking is also complex and nuanced. It can also be boring. Relying on emotion is easier, simple and straightforward.

So, for the current version of the Republican Party, it's not about policy such as climate change or repairing the nation's infrastructure; it's about anger, resentment and victimization. Individual responsibility lies not with the victims (in Trump's words "you and me"), it lies only with the perpetrators…"them."

Was it great political skills that made Trump so successful? Was it shrewd strategy that made him connect with his crowd? Judging from his behavior over the past several years--some humorous, some embarrassing, some pathetic--it's hard to believe he's capable of engineering such a successful strategy. In 2016, he had an opposition candidate who self-inflicted a wound that most likely cost Hillary Clinton the election. In short, all the stars aligned in his favor—a play into anger seething below the surface and a weak opponent.

In 2020, Trump was a known quantity. His mistakes in office were there for all too see. And he had a skilled, albeit aged, opponent who avoided glaring mistakes.

Trump succeeded because he talked to his audience in the way they think. His verbiage matched their mindset. He made anger and hatred acceptable, aired openly and publicly, and often.

His ardent loyalists accept his word as gospel. To them, all the talk about his conduct is nothing more than "noise" from the left designed to deflect from his efforts to "Make America Great Again" and to "Keep America Great." Note that he never defines what this means; it means whatever his loyalists choose it to mean, after their anger and rage is sufficiently aroused.

He has successfully aroused suspicion of the government's actions against him. To his loyalists, the House investigating committee, the FBI, the Department of Justice are all "enemies" who must be dealt with by his army of "patriots;" otherwise, they "won't have a country anymore." This is straight out of the dictator's playbook, but again, the Trumpites either don't believe this, or simply don't care. They just continue to adore their idol.

Also from this playbook is Trump's demand for complete loyalty, no questions asked. He will return loyalty, but only if he gets 100% of it from his cronies and MAGA gang. As soon as anyone begins to doubt him, or asks him questions he finds bothersome, that person becomes part of the "enemy." Trump has succeeded in removing the fence between what is proper and what is deserving of condemnation.

But Trump is also proving that he is not the best messenger for conservatism, assuming the MAGA minions are true conservatives. His rambling, sometimes incoherent message, coupled with his exposure to the criminal justice system, is taking a toll on his status as party leader.

While he's receives strong support from his cronies, that support is becoming less vigorous, and more and more are steadily peeling off.

It won't be Trump carrying the ball going forward into the future. Too many ambitious people are just standing in the wings, waiting for Trump to fail. Trumpism, however, will remain, unless broken by events yet to unfold.

A more polished, slicker version of Trump may well emerge from the ashes. That's what makes going forward beyond the November elections so intriguing. Stay tuned.

PEELING OFF FROM DONALD TRUMP

Donald Trump's former Attorney General William Barr has issued a scathing critique of a major court victory for Donald Trump in the Mar-a-Lago classified documents matter. This is leading to increased scrutiny of the Trump-appointed judge who put the brakes on the FBI's investigation.

Barr's latest attack on anything that favors Trump in his battles with the nation's criminal justice system is a continuing trend of former Trump loyalists to lukewarm supporters who have abandoned him over his aberrant conduct over the years.

Recall that Barr was a supporter of Trump's penchant for testing the limits of presidential power. Since Trump's refusal to accept his defeat to President Joe Biden in 2020, Barr has emerged as one of his most vigorous and significant critics. Barr infuriated Trump by publicly declaring there was no significant electoral fraud. And his video testimony has emerged as one of the key weapons in the televised hearings run by the House select committee investigating the attack on the capital.

As Trump continues to hold rallies to keep his base in his hip pocket as he moves toward 2024, it is important to note that he doesn't have the same level of support from top party leadership that he had when elected in 2016. Aside from his now strained relationship with Mitch McConnell, below is a partial list of those who have abandoned him, either during his term or since.

As the nation moves beyond the November midterm elections, it is important to see what these party leaders, and others who are disaffected from Trump, do to moderate the party.

Military leadership

Former Defense Secretary James Mattis==He called Trump "the first president in my lifetime who does not try to unite the American people. We are witnessing the consequences of three years without mature leadership. We must reject and hold accountable those in office who would make a mockery of our Constitution."

Former Navy Secretary Richard V. Spencer--In a Washington Post op-ed, Spencer called Trump's intervention in the war crimes case "shocking and unprecedented It was also a reminder that the President has very little understanding of what it means to be in the military, to fight ethically or to be governed by a uniform set of rules and practices."

Former White House national security adviser John Bolton--Bolton said Trump directed him to help with his pressure campaign in Ukraine to dig up dirt on Hunter Biden.

White House advisors

Former White House chief of staff John Kelly--Kelly has said he believes Bolton's accusation – that Trump told Bolton US security aid to Ukraine was conditioned on an investigation of the President's political rivals. Kelly also said he would have cautioned Trump against the idea of using law enforcement to clear Lafayette Square ahead of his photo-op outside of St. John's Church.

Former White House national security adviser H.R. McMaster--McMaster, asked if it is appropriate for a president to solicit foreign interference in the US political process, answered, "No, it's absolutely not."

Former Homeland Security adviser Tom Bossert—Bossert was "deeply disturbed" by the contents of Trump's call with the Ukrainian President. Bossert said he had told Trump there was no basis for the theory that Ukraine intervened in the 2016 US presidential election to assist Democrats. Bossert has also criticized Trump for not wearing a face mask in public amid the coronavirus pandemic. "Do as I say, not as I do isn't very useful."

Cliff Sims, former special assistant to the President and director of White House Message Strategy--Sims wrote "Team of Vipers," claiming, among other things, that Trump created an "enemies list" consisting of members of his own administration.

Omarosa Manigault Newman, former director of communications for the White House Office of Public Liaison--Manigault Newman claimed she was fired because she knew too much about a possible audio recording of Trump saying a racial epithet.

Former White House communications director Anthony Scaramucci--After Trump visited El Paso, Texas, and Dayton, Ohio, following two mass shootings, Scaramucci described the visits as a "catastrophe. For the last 3 years I have fully supported this President. Recently he has said things that divide the country in a way that is unacceptable." Scaramucci had called Trump's attacks on four minority congresswomen "racist and unacceptable."

Gary Cohn, former National Economic Council director--Cohn said last year that he was "concerned" there was no one left in Trump's staff to stand up to him and tell him what he didn't want to hear. "We had an interesting nucleus of people when I was in the White House – the initial team. We were not bashful. It was a group that was willing to tell the President what he needed to know, whether he wanted to hear it or not. None of us are there anymore. So I am concerned that the atmosphere in the White House is no longer conducive, or no one has the personality to stand up and tell the President what he doesn't want to hear."

Former White House counsel Ty Cobb--Former White House lawyer Ty Cobb's views about special counsel Robert Mueller and the Russia investigation have been at odds with the President. After leaving the White House, he said he did not think the special counsel's probe was a "witch hunt."

Trump's cabinet

Former US Ambassador to the United Nations Nikki Haley--Haley said the President's decision to remove US troops from northern Syria during Turkey's plans to launch a military offensive in the region would equate to the US leaving its Kurdish allies "to die."

Former Secretary of State Rex Tillerson--Tillerson said Russian President Vladimir Putin was more prepared than Trump for a meeting in Germany, putting American officials at a disadvantage. Tillerson also called Trump "undisciplined" and Trump would ask him to do things he didn't understand were a violation of the law.

Former US Special Representative for Ukraine Kurt Volker--He thought "it was a mistake" for Trump to try and withhold aid from Ukraine for political reasons.

Former Attorney General Jeff Sessions, who angered Trump by recusing himself from the Russia investigation. "Look, I know your anger, but recusal was required by law. I did my duty…. .. It protected the rule of law and resulted in your exonerated. Your personal feelings don't dictate who Alabama picks as their senator, the people of Alabama do."

Those who resigned over January 6

Former Transportation Secretary Elaine Chao

Former U.S. Secretary of Education Betsy DeVos

Former acting White House Chief of Staff Mick Mulvaney

Former deputy national security adviser Matt Pottinger

Former White House press secretary and chief of staff to first lady Melania Trump, **Stephanie Grisham.**

Other officials who resigned over Trump's behavior on January 6 included one of Trump's top economic advisers, Tyler Goodspeed; deputy press secretary Sarah Matthews; White House social secretary Rickie Niceta; and John Costello, a deputy assistant secretary of Commerce.

Elinore McCance-Katz, who was assistant secretary of the Department of Health and Human Services for mental health and substance use; Eric Dreiband, assistant attorney general in charge of the civil rights division; Ryan Tully, senior director for European and Russian affairs at the National Security Council; and FAA officials Arjun Garg, Brianna Manzelli, Kirk Shaffer, Bailey Edwards and Andrew Giacini also all resigned in the aftermath of January 6.

House Republicans who voted to impeach Trump

1. Rep. Liz Cheney
2. Rep. Tom Rice
3. Rep. Dan Newhouse
4. Rep. Adam Kinzinger
5. Rep. Anthony Gonzalez

6. Rep. Fred Upton
7. Rep. Jaime Herrera Beutler
8. Rep. Peter Meijer
9. Rep. John Katko
10. Rep. David Valadao

Republican Senators who voted to convict

Richard Burr, North Carolina
Bill Cassidy, Louisiana
Susan Collins, Maine
Lisa Murkowski, Alaska
Mitt Romney, Utah
Ben Sasse, Nebraska
Pat Toomey, Pennsylvania

AS THE NOVEMBER ELECTION CYCLE DRAWS NEAR, SOME FOOD FOR THOUGHT.

On the most hot-button of social issues, the Republican Party is woefully out of touch with the American public. Polls show a majority of Americans support Roe v. Wade and a majority support banning assault rifles.

Yet, the Republicans, sticking it in the eye of public opinion, fought to get a compliant Supreme Court to overturn Roe v. Wade, and vigorously oppose any further gun regulations, including an outright ban on these weapons of mass murder. In fact, Republicans are currently resisting any efforts in the courts to further limit access to firearms.

The question is why would they oppose what most Americans want. The party candidates could conceivably earn favor with more a more moderate public, helping assure themselves of greater success at the polls. Why would the party disregard those votes? The answer to both questions, it seems, lies in the strength of their base, and their perceived ability to move others to accept the right-wing agenda.

There should be no doubt about what that agenda entails. It is an obvious move to the extreme right, to the point where authoritarianism eventually replaces our almost 250-year experiment in democratic self-government.

Of course, America won't copy the form of authoritarianism as we see in Russia and China, at least initially. Sure, their leaders are "elected," but since they're really the only candidates, the election machinery is centrally controlled, and the media is under the thumb of the leader, any semblance of a fair and open election is bogus.

But once the far-right movement captures the Congress, White House and the federal courts, it's not far-fetched to see a change in the Constitution, either by Congress or a convention, to change the way presidents are chosen, and their term of office.

A constitution can provide for a democratically elected leader, or a leader in the mold of the authoritarian.

Against this backdrop, it's important to recall how authoritarianism historically gains a foothold.

Here's how editor and reporter Kevin Douglas Grant, who has led reporting projects around the world and is a student of authoritarian leaders, explains the takeover plan:

Weaponize Fear--Embrace a language of violence; promote a more punitive culture in an "us vs. them" fashion; leverage sufficient military might. Give opponents reason to believe they'll be harmed—economically at first--if they oppose. (Recall how the Republicans blame society's evils on radical leftist Democrats, saying how they'll bring socialism to America. We have had many Democratic presidents; not a single one has ever advocated a socialist society. But that doesn't matter; for Republicans, it's a great selling point.)

Target Outsiders--Stoke the fires of xenophobia by demonizing immigrants and foreigners—anyone who is different from the "us." Blame domestic problems, including economic woes, on these scapegoats and brand political opponents as supportive or at least sympathetic to these imagined enemies. (Republicans add to their rhetoric arsenal the "tax and spend" accusations, overlooking the generous gifts they hand out to the super-wealthy and big corporations. But they bank on the voters not paying attention to that.)

Undermine Institutions—Criticize the courts, then take them over by taking over the executive branch of government, whose chief executive will appoint like-minded judges; reduce checks and balances to a concept, not reality; undo established treaties and legislation that limit executive power; weaken protections for free and fair elections. (Every time Donald Trump and his ardent followers face criticism, they use this technique to undermine law enforcement, the criminal justice system, etc. as "enemies of the state" or "enemies of the people." They snub their noses and continue to egg on their supporters, hoping they'll buy the Kool-Aid. Many have.)

Rewrite History--Exert control over schools and the media to indoctrinate the public with beliefs that reinforce autocratic power. Rewrite history first by removing references to the nation's warts and failings, including book-banning, and replace it with a sanitized version that includes a heavy dose of nationalism. (Several Republican governors, notably Greg Abbott in Texas and Ron DeSantis in Florida, have been working overtime to cleanse curriculum and dictating what can and can't be taught to students. They are egging on parents and guardians to take over school districts and re-work curriculum and remove history that makes people uncomfortable.)

Exploit Religion--Appeal to the religious majority while targeting minorities. Conflate national identity with religious identity. Establish that the "us" believes in faith while the "them" are non-believers and therefore bad people. (The party's appeal to the Evangelicals is well-documented.)

Divide and Conquer--Use hate speech and encourage violent actors to widen social rifts and manufactured crises to seize more power. Repeatedly remind those who are for "the cause" that violence against "them" is a patriotic act. Repeatedly refer to your efforts as those of righteousness; your opponents are against all that is right and just. (Just listen to Trump, Kevin McCarthy, Ted Cruz, Marjorie Taylor Greene, and their ilk and this part of the playbook is glaringly evident.)

Erode Truth--Attack the press as an "enemy of the people"; dismiss negative reports as "fake news." Counter legitimate information with misinformation, or "alternative facts." Blast the media landscape with endless scandal and contradiction to overwhelm the traditional fail-safe mechanisms. To further erode the truth, add repeated, incessant lying, so that the audience becomes numb to the truth. Remember Nazi chief propagandist Joseph Goebbels' statement: a lie repeated often enough becomes the truth. Use the psychological technique of gaslighting--repeating a false narrative so often that people begin to doubt their own sense of reality or sanity. (Trump is popular despite his current legal situations because he's so effective at this. And his followers and MAGA minions eat it up like candy.)

Defend Actions in the Name of Freedom—Answer any criticism of these actions as acts of freedom. Include other feel-good buzzwords such as liberty, justice and the promotion of law and order. Attack critics as being against freedom and accompanying feel-goods. (Trump and his gubernatorial loyalists are very effective at this, labelling restrictions on voting, curriculum, classroom limits, etc., as freedom; branding Trump's unlawful taking of classified records as an exemplar of the rule of law. And on and on.)

For those with any degree of knowledge of history and governments, the evidence is as clear as a bell. Those who say there is nothing wrong with what the far-right is doing in taking over the Republican Party, they are denying what is in front of them, what is in broad daylight.

Incredibly, there are still Republicans who believe that all of the state voting changes following the 2020 presidential election were not to help Republicans get elected; rather, they were designed to prevent Democrats from cheating. This, despite more than 60 judges, including Trump appointees, concluding from his lawyers' desperate and embarrassing showing, that there was no fraud of sufficient import that would have changed the outcome of that, or any other, election that year. Even Florida Gov. Ron DeSantis said Florida's election was smooth and well run.

But there certainly were efforts to cheat in the presidential election.

We know that in Michigan, for example, poll workers were encouraged by Republican Party leaders to ignore local election rules and break them if necessary.

And we also know that part of Trump's effort to overturn the presidential election involved an effort to rig the Electoral College in seven battleground states.

On December 14, 2020, legitimate members of the Electoral College met across the country to sign certificates declaring which presidential candidate won their state. That day, in several states that Biden had won, Republicans met to sign certificates declaring that they were the "duly elected and qualified" members of the Electoral College and falsely declaring Trump the winner of their state. They sent their documents to the National Archives.

In the runup to January 6, 2021, these false certificates were used in an effort to claim that Vice President Mike Pence could decide either not to recognize any electors from these "disputed states" (meaning an outright Trump win) or else delay the certification of the election.

None of the voting law changes in Republican-controlled states dealt with these two graphic examples of cheating.

If there was any additional cheating, it was done by the Russians who helped Trump get elected. So say the unanimous conclusion of our intelligence agencies.

But some people will believe anything that fits their mindset. The facts be damned.

Here is another graphic example of how Republicans are calling censorship freedom, straight out of the authoritarian's playbook. As CNN reports, "Dozens of books have been pulled from shelves in Texas, new policies expanding oversight of books are being drafted or already passed in multiple states, a Florida school district halted library purchases and a teacher resigned in Oklahoma over the censorship of books in classroom libraries.

With new laws that restrict teaching about race, history and gender identity in effect in more than a dozen states, students are starting to see changes in the classroom and more might be coming in the next months.

In a recent analysis, the literary and free expression advocacy organization PEN America found that 19 states have laws targeting discussions of race, gender, and United States history; and 36 other states introduced 137 similar bills in 2022, marking a significant increase compared to the 54 bills proposed last year."

By any legitimate definition, this isn't freedom; it's pure censorship by government. This isn't liberty; it's control of what people can think or say.

This is precisely why the next two elections are so essential for the well-being of our nation. In November of this year, voters will decide which party controls the Congress, and the legislative agenda, for the next two years. If it's the Republican Party, whatever draconian legislation proposed will meet with Joe Biden's veto pen.

But the focus immediately following November will be 2024. If the Republicans gain Congress, they will move heaven and earth to take the White House. If the Democrats take one or both houses of Congress, The Republicans will sharpen their knives to oust the Democrats in 2024, albeit from a far weakened position. Not that that will deter them.

If the Republicans are successful this year and in 2024, they will make every effort to take over control of the federal judiciary.

Philosopher Jason Stanley of Yale University, best known for his 2018 book How Fascism Works, says "Once you have the courts you can pretty much do whatever you want."

Read that last sentence again. We are indeed two elections away.

PAY ATTENTION TO THIS CASE BEFORE THE SUPREME COURT; IT MAY CHANGE FOREVER HOW PRESIDENTS AND LEGISLATIVE REPRESENTATIVES ARE CHOSEN.

When there is any general public discussion of a Supreme Court case, it's usually on an emotionally charged issue such as abortion, gun control, religious freedom, etc. When a case involves nuanced legal issues, there is a tendency to leave any discussion to the lawyers; the general public isn't that interested in such things.

Pay attention to this case now pending before the Court. It could change the way presidents, as well as state legislatures and members of the U.S. House of Representatives are chosen in a most draconian, anti-Democratic way. Author and historian Heather Cox Richardson devoted her column yesterday to this case.

The case is Moore v. Harper.

The issue before the Court is whether state legislatures alone have the power to set election rules even if those laws violate the state constitutions. Republicans argue that the state court can't prevent the legislatures from making these ultimate decisions because of the "independent state legislature doctrine."

This position is based on the clause in the federal Constitution that says "[t]he Times, Places and Manner of holding Elections for Senators and Representatives, shall be prescribed in each State by the Legislature thereof; but the Congress may at any time by Law make or alter such Regulations."

Richardson says, "(u)ntil now, states have interpreted "legislatures" to mean the state's general lawmaking processes, which include shared power and checks and balances among the three branches of state government. Now a radical minority insists that a legislature is a legislature alone, unchecked by state courts or state constitutions that prohibit gerrymandering."

While those Republicans who advocate for the independent state legislature theory so they can gerrymander their state legislative and congressional districts, there is also a more draconian reason behind their efforts before the conservative-majority Supreme Court:, they cite another clause of the Constitution that says: "Each State shall appoint, in such Manner as the Legislature thereof may direct, a Number of Electors."

They advance the theory that the legislature also can ultimately choose the state's presidential electors regardless of which candidate the majority of the state's voters choose. In other words, regardless of the popular vote totals of the presidential candidates, it is the legislature that makes the final decision on the state's electors. Candidate A could receive a majority of the popular vote, but if the state legislature is controlled by the opposing party, the legislature can award all the state's electoral votes to the losing candidate B.

Those who support the current method of electing the president, not by direct popular vote, but by choosing the winning candidate's electors by popular vote in each state, find this theory appalling because it has the operational effect of nullifying the popular vote if the state legislature so decides.

This "independent state legislature" theory is what Trump and his allies pushed for to keep him in office in 2020 despite having lost the popular vote by more than seven million.

Trump's lawyers argued that Republican state legislatures could have tossed out the will of the people in key states and send Trump electors to Congress for certification by the vice president rather than the Biden electors voted for by the majority.

When a case reaches the Supreme Court, the Court typically receives what are called amicus, or "friend of the court," briefs from both sides. Although these briefs are supposed to assist the Court in its deliberations, usually they serve the purpose of advocating for a particular result. It's a form of lobbying, judicial lobbying.

Richardson notes the flood of these friend of the court briefs that have been coming into the Court, each one advocating for their side in this vitally important constitutional law case.

As Richardson notes: "Not surprisingly, those writing friend of the court briefs defending the independent state legislature doctrine are a who's who of those who backed Trump's effort to convince state officials to write slates of electors for Trump rather than Biden. They include America First Legal Foundation, which Democracy Docket identifies as connected to Trump advisor Stephen Miller and Trump's chief of staff Mark Meadows; America's Future (Trump's national security advisor Michael Flynn); Claremont Institute's Center for Constitutional Jurisprudence (John

Eastman, author of the Eastman memo for overturning the 2020 election); Honest Elections Project (Leonard Leo); Public Interest Legal Foundation (Eastman and Trump lawyer Cleta Mitchell), Restoring Integrity and Trust in Elections (Trump's attorney general Bill Barr), and so on."

This is indeed a who's who of extreme right-wing lawyers.

"In contrast, a conference consisting of the Supreme Court chief justices or chief judges of the courts of last resort of all 50 states, the District of Columbia, Puerto Rico, the Northern Mariana Islands, American Samoa, Guam, and the Virgin Islands, (are) urg(ing) the Supreme Court not to decide that the state legislatures could operate without any oversight. Relying on the long history of state court review of the legislatures' decisions, including those over elections, (this group) concluded that state courts had a traditional role to play in reviewing election laws under state constitutions," she writes.

"Revered conservative judge J. Michael Luttig has been trying for months to sound the alarm that the independent state legislature doctrine is a blueprint for Republicans to steal the 2024 election. In April, before the court agreed to take on the Moore v. Harper case, he wrote: 'Trump and the Republicans can only be stopped from stealing the 2024 election at this point if the Supreme Court rejects the independent state legislature doctrine…and Congress amends the Electoral Count Act to constrain Congress' own power to reject state electoral votes and decide the presidency.'"

Here is where the rubber meets the road in this case: in a case decided earlier this year on redistricting, four conservative justices--Samuel Alito, Neil Gorsuch, Clarence Thomas, and Brett Kavanaugh---signaled they are open to the notion that state courts have no role in overseeing the rules for federal elections.

Richardson concludes, "In the one term Trump's three justices have been on the court, they have decimated the legal landscape under which we have lived for generations, slashing power from the federal government, where Congress represents the majority, and returning it to states, where a Republican minority can impose its will. Thanks to the skewing of our electoral system, those states are now trying to take control of our federal government permanently."

Is there any doubt in anyone's mind where the current version of the Republican Party wants to take the country?

HERE IS THE CENTRAL PROBLEM RESULTING FROM THE FEDERAL JUDGE'S DECISION TO APPOINT A SPECIAL MASTER TO REVIEW RECORDS REMOVED FROM TRUMP'S RESIDENCE.

The federal judge's decision to appoint a special master requested by Donald Trump's lawyers raises many questions going forward.

You recall the FBI, armed with a lawfully executed probable cause affidavit, obtained a search warrant from a federal magistrate to enter Trump's resort for the purpose of seizing classified documents he took from the White House and sequestered them at Mar-a-Lago.

After the predictable legal battle between his lawyers and those of the Department of Justice, the Trump-appointed judge sided with the ex-president, saying his situation is unique, and there is a risk to his reputation should some of the documents, which should remain private, become public.

Two issues immediately came to mind. First, considering the state of Trump's reputation, whether anything additional disclosures would further harm his reputation is viewed with great skepticism by some many legal experts, including those who served in his administration. The fact is despite everything we know about him, people either love him or despise him, with no or very little grounds in between.

Second, federal magistrates have duties provided by law, as well as those assigned by a federal judge. Those assigned duties include holding hearings and determining any non-case-dispositive pretrial matter, such as procedural and discovery motions. While there is no criminal proceeding pending before the court, this amply demonstrates that federal magistrates are well-equipped to review large volumes of documents and issue rulings on them.

In this regard, what makes a private attorney/special master better able to do what a federal magistrate does as a matter of course, remains unanswered. Perhaps one of the judge's considerations is to take the pressure off the magistrates, especially considering the threats against the one who issued the warrant. If that's the case, the appointment certainly accomplishes that. Whether any lawyer wants to risk threats of violence by taking on the special master role and issuing a ruling Trump doesn't like is worth considering.

The first problem concerns the organization of the documents seized by the FBI. Reports to date note that at least some classified records were mixed with others that appear personal and of no interest to the FBI; others that might harm Trump's reputation; others that might involve attorney-client privilege; and still others that might involve executive privilege. Reports further note that some documents were strewn about the property, not kept in individual boxes.

The first step in collecting, collating and organizing the mass of documents is to place them in some identifiable order.

There are three levels of classification defined by federal law; Top Secret, Secret, and Confidential.

Documents are classified and organized through a seven-step process: complete a risk assessment of sensitive data; develop a formalized classification policy; categorize the types of data; discover the location of the data; identify and classify data; enable controls of the information; and monitor and maintain securely.

There are also several sub-steps that must be followed through each of these seven steps. It's a time-consuming process, making sure the right level of classification is given to each document and secured and maintained according to its appropriate level.

That process was concluded before Trump removed the boxes from the White House. However, it is possible that as the mass of documents are reviewed by the special master, he or she will have to number them so that order will be made of the disorder the FBI found.

When I practiced law and had to deal with voluminous records, I used a well-established numbering system knows as Bates numbering, or Bates stamping. This system is used in the legal, medical, and business fields to place one or more identifying numbers, date and time marks on documents as they are scanned or processed, for example, during the discovery stage of preparations for trial or identifying business receipts. Whether this, or a similar system, will be used on classified records remains to be seen, but it is an issue in getting a handle on this mass of documents.

An offshoot of this concern is actually putting an identifier on a classified document. It is conceivable that adding anything to a classified document, even an identifying number, could compromise the document should it be necessary for use in a criminal trial. Documents that have to pass through many hands raise what is known as a chain of command issue. It's possible that each person handling a record could change it from its original form. Highly unlikely as a practical matter in this instance, still, remember a lawyer whose purpose is to delay will resort to any argument that furthers that goal. Claiming alteration of a document certainly serves that purpose.

A second problem is who also gets access to these records. If a federal magistrate were in charge, court personnel would presumably be available to assist in the process. But for a special master from the private sector, the question arises whether that person will be able to use private staff in the examination-organization process.

The more people who access classified information, the greater the risk of a leak, which could compromise sources, threaten national security and put others at great personal peril. Already, we know the FBI and the federal magistrate who issued the warrant have been threatened by right-wing groups. And as noted previously, there's that "too many hands" issue.

Once the battle between the Trump lawyers and Department of Justice lawyers over the selection of the special master is resolved, and the battle over document organization is settled (who knows how long that might take), the problem then becomes how objections to individual documents will be handled.

It's obvious that the process will be contentious. What is considered by the FBI to be classified in any one of the three levels could well be objected to by Trump's lawyers. They could conceivably argue that a given document was misclassified, leading to battle over battle over hundreds of records.

Then there's the prospect of vigorous disagreement over whether a document is personal, protected by the attorney-client privilege, and/or covered by executive privilege. On the latter, there has never been a case where a former president exerted executive privilege over documents created while in office. Assuming this issue arises before the special master and the federal judge, two questions will no doubt arise: whether a former president can claim this privilege when a sitting president doesn't, and whether the document in question is covered by that privilege. The first question will no doubt go to the Supreme Court if the case gets that far.

Still, the prospect of each document having to face argument of counsel, a disputed decision, review by the presiding judge and the high prospect of an appeal will no doubt slow down the process immeasurably, unless the court can come up with a streamlined, simplified method of dealing with the anticipated contentiousness, such as combining all objections and rulings in a single omnibus order that can be appealed.

Recall the old adage; justice delayed is justice denied. The process of moving these records from seizure to examination to categorization to proper placement (personal, privilege protected) to use by the FBI to complete its investigation, could take many months. Any criminal prosecution could be well down the road—months, perhaps even years.

Which is precisely what Trump wants.

DONALD TRUMP'S LAMENT: "IT'S THOSE %$#@% DEMOCRATS' FAULT"

Everything was perfect. In 2017, after my landslide victory over Crooked Hillary, I was ready to become the greatest president in American history and everybody would know it. Well, at least today my MAGA crowd knows the truth: I am the greatest POTUS ever! They should take down someone's head from Mount Rushmore and replace it with mine!

It's those lousy evil Democrats who attacked me; they even turned some former real Republicans into Democrats. Those miserable RINOs. Those vicious Never-Trumpers! They will never understand what a great man I am.

It's those radical libs that made me say there were some wonderful white nationalists and neo-Nazis in Charlottesville back in 2017, even though there were. It's those Antifas and other radicals that are the real enemy. The others were just doing their patriotic duty defending real Americans. But I get blamed for everything, so I guess this was just another chance to make me look bad.

Then they blamed me for weakly dealing with COVID. But I showed my usual incredible strength. I thought it was a pretty good idea to drink a disinfectant to get rid of it, to make it go away. Those horrible people, and some of the media, too--- those enemies of the people--said I made people drink bleach. Actually, people could have chosen any other disinfectant if they wanted to. I mean, that's real freedom, isn't it? Believe me when I tell you I know what real freedom is.

And about that phone call to Ukraine. The one that those un-American House Democrats ganged up on me on and had the nerve to impeach me. Fortunately, those wonderful House and Senate Republicans stood by me. These real Republicans will always be there for me. If not, I'll just find some what the Dems call weirdo wacko candidates to run against those who dare to challenge my word or deed.

Well, it was a perfect call. All it was was one president chatting with another. I was told Congress was sending them some money, so it was just natural of me, being such a great social person that I am, to call my fellow president and politely ask if he had any information about Hunter Biden that I might find useful. I know Biden had some action there, so, well, what the heck. I mean, I was running against his evil father and I thought there just might be something there. Typically, the lamestream media and the socialist Democrats made it out that I was looking for dirt in exchange for the money. How silly is that! Well, Ukraine finally got the money after that call and the chicken was out of the coop. But to say this was, what do they call it, a quid pro quo, well that's just a foreign language to me. I'm an American; talk American to me!

Now, let me say something about that election in 2020. Everyone knows I won fair and square. I know over 60 judges disagreed with me; now most Americans disagree with me. What did those judges really know? They're not as smart as me. I know some of them are my appointees; well, you can't be perfect all the time I suppose. And we know those people who disagree with me were brainwashed by Democrats and the liberal media. It's good to know that Americans can trust the real Republicans to see through the brainwashing and tell the people the truth.

My loyal supporters in government and those MAGA folks know the truth. I tell them the truth now every time I'm on my beloved Truth Social. They know they can believe what I tell them. They know the lamestream media and the Democrats are in cahoots to tear me down. I alone always tell the truth.

Let me tell you the truth about January 6. On that day, I told my loyal supporters, those true patriots, that they wouldn't have a country anymore if those evil Democrats got away with stealing the election. I was ready to lead them on a march to the Capitol, but was blocked from doing that.

It was Antifa all along dressed as my supporters that stormed the building. Until it wasn't, but then it was obvious it was just some of my dedicated patriots who expressed their discontent over those stolen election results and peacefully protested at the Capitol. That's the American way. It was those wicked Democrats and their media friends that made it appear that my people were rioting and destroying property. I know a few died, but it's all on their heads, not mine.

Then these despicable people had the nerve to impeach me again over that. Even more RINOs joined the #%$& Democrats. But in the end, I was found not guilty. Well, that's what I was told when the Senate refused to convict.

Not to be outdone, the House set up a witch hunt committee to investigate that peaceful protest, and even got Republicans who worked with me in the White House to become RINOs and testify against me. All lies, and they were under oath! Of course, I've never testified under oath, and never will. You just don't know how they could twist what I say and make it seem like I'm lying.

If that wasn't enough, they're making a big stink over a few boxes of what they say are highly classified records that I took to my home in Mar-a-Lago. Well, how am I supposed to write my memoirs without them? And besides, you can't trust those Democrats to protect these records, and where better would they be safe than with me?

The FBI said these so-called secret records were mixed up with other stuff. We know the FBI has been weaponized by Biden and his crew. That's something I would have never done; I don't care what Jim Comey or any other ex-FBI official says. I'm glad I fired him for refusing to be loyal to me. Besides, have you ever had to move from one home to another in a short time? I mean, I was forced by those evil people to rush packing up my stuff and leave town. Of course some stuff got mixed up with others, but I knew where everything was, even if some stuff was found on the floor where guests and others can freely view my magnificent resort.

Remember, I'm the stable genius. I alone can fix it, and that means anything and everything. As for all those records, well, they belong to me. I had them in the White House when I lived there, and I took what was there that belonged to me and brought them to my beautiful Florida home. You should see all the gold. Moved them from one home to another. People do that every day. Nothing wrong with that.

I don't know why folks continue to blame me for what they say I said or did over the past few years. I've been blamed for so many things; I'll tell you, it's all part of the biggest hoax and witch hunt ever. I'm the most persecuted president in history. So what if all this persecution is because of things they say I did; we know it was all their fault. They are trying to destroy the perfect man that I am and that you see before your very eyes.

I'm a big believer in being held accountable for your actions. Well, they should be held accountable for theirs. I don't need to be held accountable because I've done nothing wrong.

I mean, when all is said and done, who you gonna believe, me or your lying eyes..and ears?

All I want is another chance in the White House to continue the great things that I've done to Make America Great Again and what I will do to Keep America Great. You'll see that I will do even greater things that what I did before. The hoaxes and witch hunts won't stop me. The Democrats won't stop me. The RINOs won't stop me. Nothing will stop me. With your continued loyalty no matter what others say, I will work for you.

Believe me.

THE MYTH THAT INFLATION IS ALL BIDEN'S FAULT.

There are those on the right who, in reliance on "if-then" explanations for our nation's problem, gleefully point to rising costs and blame the Biden Administration for inflation. In short, their view is if we have inflation, then it's because of the Biden Administration's policies. This approach is both simple, and simplistic. Offering a simple, and thereby flawed, explanation to answer a complex question is a disservice to the public. It doesn't educate; it plays into ignorance.

Books have been written by economists on the subjects of inflation, recession, depression, and deflation, among others. And as with any other academic endeavor, experts do disagree.

But with regard to inflation over the past year or so, there is general agreement that two distinct causes must added to the usual causes of inflation.

First, the COVID pandemic played a leading role in the jump in inflation as lingering COVID-induced supply chain disruptions made it difficult to find some items while driving up consumer prices.

Second, the Russian invasion of Ukraine was the principal cause of higher inflation, comprising 3.5% of the 8.6%. Oil and commodities prices jumped in anticipation of and response to the invasion, leading to higher gasoline prices.

These two causes can't be overlooked or downplayed; they had and have a significant effect on the nation's economy.

Now to the usual causes of inflation. Generally, there are two main causes of inflation are:

"Demand-pull inflation occurs in a strong economy. Incomes are increasing, people are being paid more, more people are at work, and they are demanding more goods and services. This decreases the total number of goods and services available—more people can afford the limited supply of existing goods and services. This, in turn, raises prices. In general, some demand-pull inflation is a sign of a functioning economy, as people are working and earning enough money to demand everything that's produced.

Cost-push inflation is caused by an increase in the cost of goods due to causes on the supply end. For example, if the costs of raw materials go up significantly, and businesses cannot keep up production of manufactured goods, this causes the manufactured goods sold at the market to be more expensive.

Natural disasters, pandemics, and rising oil prices may all result in cost-push inflation, for example. Many different economic conditions can result in cost-push inflation, and it's something policymakers may worry about, as cost-push inflation can be difficult to rein in."

With rising prices, voters are naturally angry at the party in power. The anger over this issues fuels a backlash against the party in power, which by default favors the party out of power.

Why are prices so high? Avoiding a knee-jerk answer to a complex matter, focus on the supply-and-demand cycle. When demand is high, prices go up. When demand is low, prices go down in the hopes of spurring greater demand. Should that increase in demand materialize, what happens to prices? They go up. High demand, high prices. Low demand, low prices.

Remember that businesses are ultimately geared toward one overarching end: profits. If businesses lose money, chances are they won't be in business very long. Breaking even may be ok, but over the long haul, breaking even isn't financially sustainable.

If the product or service that is offered is of sufficient quality, people will buy to the level they can afford, perhaps even going in debt to make the purchase. People are by nature consumers, and businesses depend on consumption.

The importance of purchasing power can't be overstated. Republicans, however, generally oppose a set minimum wage that produces a livable income. They believe that increasing the minimum wage works against businesses' bottom line. They believe that greater profits will result in greater investment. We all know the history of trickle-down economics: profits take precedence over investment.

When government pumps money into the economy, such as passing legislation to repair and maintain our infrastructure, or address climate change, businesses engaged in this line of work will most likely hire new employees. There may even be promotions with higher salaries. The new employees will become consumers. The ones promoted will be able to consume more. In sum, they will be able to buy more products and services. What will happen to the costs of those products and services occasioned by this increased demand? You know the answer to that.

With regard to a higher minimum wage, business opposition remains even though they are quite capable of passing along those increases to the consumer. But businesses have to be careful not to price themselves out of the market.

This is the great balancing act businesses must adhere to. A product's or service's price must be attractive enough to assure a positive bottom line, yet not be so high as to be largely unaffordable.

Since government can't force or control demand, and doesn't set prices, it can't raise or lower them. But through certain federal actions, like the Federal Reserve lowering or increasing interest rates, the government can influence prices, which in turn will influence demand.

Businesses favor the Republican Party. Republicans provide for a better business climate by generally opposing those programs proffered by Democrats that provide benefits for the vast majority of Americans--including Republicans of course—such as health care, social programs, dealing with climate change and environmental issues, infrastructure repair and maintenance, etc.

What businesses can do in Machiavellian manner is create an environment where demand is heightened, such as keeping products from reaching the market for eventual sale. Recall those container ships stalled in the waters off the coast. Was this a deliberate act? Recall when gasoline products were withheld from the sellers.

The ultimate question on this point is whether there is some form of understanding between the Republican Party and Big Business that, in return for favorable action such as tax benefits, Big Business will create conditions that could spur inflation. We'll leave that one for the experts.

The point here is that ours is a managed economy, and businesses are quite capable of doing their part in the management process.

The classic line is applicable here: follow the money. The unprecedented level of corporate profits while consumers suffer from rising costs applies to the oil companies; just check out the various sites for information on Big Oil profits as gas prices soared.

The bottom line is there are those making a financial killing out of inflation. what is being done to rein in these huge profits at the expense of the consumers? Congress can act, but there are members of Congress who either support soaring corporate profits, or simply turn a blind eye to them.

CHIEF JUSTICE ROBERTS SAYS SUPREME COURT'S LEGITIMACY MUST NOT BE QUESTIONED. NONSENSE.

Chief Justice John Roberts says it's ok to question the Court's opinions, but not its legitimacy. And how exactly are people to judge the Court's legitimate role in our society? By its opinions, of course. If judicial opinions are out of sync with public opinion, the Court opens itself up to having its basic legitimacy questioned.

He says the Court is not a political instrument; yet he need only look to the heated ideological battles in the senate over the past several years that put the current justices on the bench. Does Roberts honestly believe that once on the Court, the five hand-picked right-wing ideologists who have a reading of the Constitution at odds with others, are going to become something entirely different?

Someone needs to inform the Chief Justice of William Shakespeare's famous line from "Julius Caesar," "The fault lies not in our stars, but in ourselves." The Court is responsible for its own actions; it is not the people's fault for questioning it. The justices need to show a little of that individual responsibility they champion.

THE MYTHS OF REPUBLICANS' "WHATABOUTISM" AND "THEY'RE ALL THE SAME." AND OTHER MYTHS FROM THE RIGHT.

Whenever Donald Trump or his diehard loyalists in government are accused of some wrongdoing, the response from their supporters is usually one of the two noted above.

The myth about "whataboutism" has been repeatedly exposed, and even some of the Republicans who've had enough of Trump and Trumpism are backing off this one. And there is a good reason for that.

“Whataboutism is usually voiced as “What about Hillary?” and “What about Hunter Biden?” First, they don’t compare to what Trump and his cronies have done. Neither lied about the 2020 election nor led an assault on the capital. Neither sought dirt on an opposition candidate in return for appropriated funds. Neither illegally removed government records nor stored them in his home. Neither was a president of the United States. Second, the Republicans had every opportunity to charge Clinton when the party controlled Congress and the White House from 2017-2019, but even Trump’s Justice Department realized they didn’t have a case against her. As for Biden, he is currently under investigation by a Trump-appointed federal prosecutor.

So much for the juvenile “whataboutism” nonsense. About the best thing that can be said about those who still believe this is “there are none so blind as they who will not see.”

Now for the second myth right-wing defenders rely on: they’re all the same. That is, the radicals on the left are as dangerous as the radicals on the right. It’s a form of “whataboutism,” but when people have no facts, they’ll throw anything against the wall hoping something sticks. Besides, our national security agencies have unanimously concluded that the greatest threat to our county is from right wing extremists, so “whataboutism” here is another myth.

Asked to identify the radicals on the left, chances are the first person named by the right is Alexandria Ocasio-Cortez of New York. She and her so-called "gang of four" in the House of Representatives are usually the culprits the right conveniently single out as examples of radical extremists. In the senate, it's usually Bernie Sanders of Vermont. Ask those on the right to identify others, and they have a tough time. Ask them what it is about these legislators that make them radicals, the usual line is: "they want socialism." They say this as if this one word sums up the so-called welfare state, which doesn't exist.

We've had lots of Democrat congressmen and -women over the years. Not a single one of them has ever instituted socialism in America. We've had lots of Democrat presidents—Franklin Roosevelt, Harry Truman, John Kennedy, Lyndon Johnson, Jimmy Carter, Bill Clinton, Barack Obama and Joe Biden. Not a single one of them brought socialism to America.

Even when Democrats controlled Congress and the White House, they never brought socialism to our shores. Those who know anything about history will recall FDR's New Deal and call that socialism. They don't understand the difference between socialist type programs and socialism as a form of government. If it weren't for those social programs, our nation might not have survived the Great Depression brought about by 12 years of Republican pro-business policies. Conservatives don't want to talk about that.

The right will point to Medicaid as a socialist program because benefits are given to those who didn't contribute to its funding. The Medicaid program is jointly funded by the federal and state governments, and at least 50 percent of each state's Medicaid funding is matched by the federal government, although the exact percentage varies by state. Medicaid is the largest source of federal funding that states receive.

The following welfare programs are offered in the U.S.: Medicaid, supplemental security income, supplemental nutrition assistance program, child's health insurance program, temporary assistance for needy families, housing assistance, and the earned income tax credit.

The fact that these programs exists, however, doesn't mean we will become a socialist country if the Democrats have their way. If that were true, we would have become a socialist country a long time ago. With regard to every named president above, programs that were initiated resulted directly from a crisis that the country faced at the time.

With regard to these few welfare programs, there are Republican myths that surround them as well. First, contrary to the notion that only Democrat states receive welfare benefits, the Tax Foundation and Gallup polls show that many of the states that rely the most on federal benefits vote Republican. Second, most are unaware that children make up the biggest percentage of welfare beneficiaries.

An examination of the demographics of welfare recipients reveals that those under the age of 18 account for 41% of all welfare users. Meanwhile, people aged between 18 and 64 account for 50% of the recipients. I'm sure Republicans wouldn't want to go on record as denying needed benefits to children.

Many voters who decry welfare programs also may not be aware of how much they receive from government programs. For example, they may not be aware that the deduction for home mortgage interest is a form of government benefit.

It's easier to consider only visible federal benefits, such as welfare checks or food stamps. As a result, many voters don't realize that they are getting government benefits too. In normal times, social welfare is vital to society. For example, social insurance, such as unemployment benefits, create a risk-sharing economy in which the threat of potential economic difficulties befalling any one person is protected by the majority.

Another myth accuses undocumented immigrants of coming to the America to take advantage of welfare programs. Most welfare programs, though, only benefit legal immigrants.

Now that the welfare myth has been exploded, the final myth concerns what the radical left wants to take from us vs. what the radical right has already taken, and threaten to take even more.

First, there is the myth of equal numbers on both side. The myth here is part of the right's mindset designed to equate the number on the extreme left with number on the extreme right, particularly in Congress. We know of the "gang of four" and Bernie Sanders on the extreme left; on the extreme right, however, we have 147 House members who voted against certifying the 2020 election, and about 15 Republican senators. I realize this is anecdotal, but in the absence of clearly established raw numbers, this is the best we have going forward. Clearly, the far right is more numerous than the far left, at least in Congress.

I don't recall anyone on the extreme left who wants to diminish voting rights, restrict civil rights, ban books, control classroom teachings, eliminate certain curriculum, or who threaten government officials when they do their jobs. In short, I don't recall anything the extreme left wants to take from anyone. Well, I'm in error on one count: there's that corporate welfare, those super-wealthy corporate donors to Republican causes, that the left is after. They can certainly afford to pay their fair share and help fund such programs that benefit everyone, like infrastructure and climate change. This is corporate welfare the right doesn't want the party faithful to discuss. They get permanent tax cuts; the middle class gets tax cuts that expire in a few years.

We have a clear picture of what the Republicans have taken away, and what they further threaten to take away. They have been boasting about this.

Republicans, knowing how people vote by group, have tamped down the opportunities to vote for certain demographics. They have successfully eliminated a woman's right to choose, and threaten to eliminate a person's right to ingest contraceptives and freely choose who they wish to marry. We further know the right threatens to eliminate the right of privacy across the board.

The Republicans have successfully banned books, eliminated subjects from school and college curriculum, and prohibited the teaching of certain subjects that might cause psychological discomfort. Their theme song should be "Don't Worry, Be Happy."

And we also know that some on the extreme right have threatened, and continue to threaten, law enforcement, FBI, federal judges, and anyone else who does their job and hold certain people accountable for violating the law.

This, from the party of law and order and the rule of law.

The bottom line here is the extreme left seeks to take nothing from the American citizen; the extreme right wants to trash several fundamental principles of Democracy like freedom of speech, freedom of thought, the unfettered equal right to vote, etc., from us. And they are succeeding.

All in the name of freedom and liberty, of course.